Liberal Adult Education

The End of an Era?

Liberal Adult Education

The End of an Era?

Edited by

John Wallis

CONTINUING EDUCATION PRESS, UNIVERSITY OF NOTTINGHAM

First published in 1996 by
Continuing Education Press
Department of Continuing Education
Education Building
University Park
Nottingham NG7 2RD

ISBN 1 85041 081 X

Printed in Great Britain by Antony Rowe Ltd

Contents

Notes on contributors

David Alexander is Senior Lecturer in Continuing Education, University of Edinburgh.

Paula Allman is Senior Lecturer in the Department of Continuing Education, University of Nottingham.

Richard Edwards is Senior Lecturer in Post-Compulsory Education, The Open University.

Desmond Keegan is a Lecturer at University College, Dublin. He was formerly Director-General of the Italian Distance University System.

Kenneth Lawson is a Special Professor in the Department of Continuing Education, University of Nottingham.

John McIlroy is Reader in Sociology, University of Manchester.

R.W.K. Paterson is Senior Lecturer in the Department of Philosophy, University of Hull.

Richard Taylor is Director of the Department of Adult Continuing Education, University of Leeds.

Jane Thompson is Tutor in Women's Studies, Ruskin College, Oxford.

Robin Usher is Senior Lecturer in Post-Compulsory Education, University of Southampton.

John Wallis is Senior Lecturer in the Department of Continuing Education, University of Nottingham.

Preface

This collection of essays was brought together for a number of reasons. Firstly, 1995 marked the seventy-fifth anniversary of the Department of Adult Education at the University of Nottingham. Established as the first Department of Adult Education, Nottingham has exhibited and exhibits a deep and cherished commitment to the British liberal tradition of university adult education.

Secondly, the essays serve as a tribute to four former colleagues who held chairs in the Nottingham department: Robert Peers, Alan Thornton, Harold Wiltshire and Michael Stephens. Historically they saw the establishment, growth and academic acceptance of university-based liberal education for adults. Their promotion and fierce defence of the service could be found in their written work and their tireless support for all forms of provision, and although these essays draw primarily on the work of Harold Wiltshire the spirit that informs the debate was common to them all. If we are at the end of an era, their contribution to its construction and dominant values deserves recognition.

Finally, it was felt that a consideration of the position of liberal adult education might be timely as its future appears to be so gravely under threat. The recent stress on the 'vocationalising' of all forms of education — whether compulsory or voluntary — has had a major impact on the adult education service. At the level of higher education the economic imperative to re-organise what were liberal extra-mural programmes into credit bearing units relating to the internal university structures is but one example of a wider trend. The impoverishment of the Local Authorities, the strict regulatory systems of the Further Education Funding Council and the Training and Enterprise Councils, and the pressure on voluntary agencies provide a landscape where opportunities appear extremely restricted. Although presented within a discourse of individual development, access and equal opportunity many feel that educational opportunities for adults are becoming de-intellectualised, reduced to a form of crude behaviourism, typified by the worst excesses of the National Vocational Qualification system. In such circumstances 'personal growth' is re-defined as the acquisition of fragmented units and competences, kept in standardised records of achievement, the latter to be used as evidence in the labour market for personal advancement. In such circumstances 'homo sapiens' is reduced to 'homo economicus'.

It is easy to dismiss recent social policy as an educational reflection of late capital's need to re-structure the labour force in light of the globalisation of world trade, and the need for more flexible and compliant workers. The simpler alternative is to discuss such changes as the philistine tendencies of the neo-liberal conservatism ushered in by the Thatcher regime. However, an equally powerful challenge to the liberal position has emerged from within the academy itself with the rise of postmodernist thought. It is not possible here to discuss the phenomenon at length, but the claims of postmodernists that the universal 'truths' are no longer valid, and that faith in the 'grand narratives' that have informed the liberal project has been misplaced, entirely undermine the basic principles of liberal adult education. Any truth — whether emerging from the Enlightenment's faith in the application of human reason, or a trust in Marxist dialectics — is discredited, and all that is left is relativism at best or meaninglessness and pessimism at worst.

It should be said that some have embraced such analysis, in that they have interpreted the smashing of the dominant paradigms as liberatory. The 'silenced' voices — by nature of gender, ethnicity, ability etc. — can now be heard in their own right. Difference is to be celebrated. In some cases the human subject, the central feature of liberal principles, is revealed as a social construct, for some locked in an endless web of discursive regimes, for others capable of creating or re-creating itself in myriad forms, which need have no inherent consistency.

The final area where these changes have impacted on the liberal tradition has been in the relationship between the education of mature people and democracy. Throughout its history liberal adult education has accepted an overt democratic intention. At a basic level, by increasing the educational 'standard' of the members of a democracy the quality of political life should be improved. For more 'radical' thinkers educational endeavour should aim to improve the possibilities of those denied active involvement in the democratic process, and to enable them to become more positively engaged. Recent pressures to present education as a 'value free' activity, and the withdrawal of economic support from all but the most extreme cases of 'special' social need, has put this element under severe threat.

So far, this introduction has made assumptions about a common understanding of the term 'liberal adult education'. For the purposes of this book contributors were directed to what has become a seminal essay by Harold Wiltshire. 'The great tradition in university adult education'. First appearing in 1956, the piece outlined very clearly the basic assumptions that informed the work at Nottingham for many years. The piece has not been re-printed, here but its key elements are outlined below:

i)   It is committed to a particular curriculum, to the humane or liberal studies (which I take to mean those studies which can reasonably be expected to concern us as men and women, not as technicians, functionaries or examinees).

ii) Within this curriculum particular concern is shown for the social studies and for those aspects of other studies which illuminate man as a social rather than a solitary being; its interest is not in learning for learning's sake but in learning as a means of under-standing the great issues of life, and its typical student is not the scholar, the solitary, the scientist or the saint; its typical student is the reflective citizen.

iii) It demands from these students a particular attitude — the non-vocational attitude — towards their studies, and therefore exami-nations and awards, which imply and encourage other attitudes, are deplored.

iv) It combines democratic notions about equality of educational opportunity with what may seem to us to be unwarrantably optimistic assumptions about the educability of normal adults and as a result rejects any attempt to select students for adult education either by examination or by reference to previous education; the only selection used is self-selection, and it is as-sumed that if you are interested enough to attend the course and competent enough to meets its demands then you are a suitable student.

v)   It adopts what may be called the Socratic method as its character-istic one, and has found in small tutorial groups meeting for guided discussion over a fairly long period its most effective educational technique (pp. 31-2).

Even at the time of writing Wiltshire recognised that his position could be seen as extreme, and largely outdated — echoing back to the altruistic values of the nineteenth century extra-mural pioneers. He clearly recognised that his stance could be casually dismissed '... desperately unmodish, something woolly-minded and crassly optimistic, something provincial and essentially slack, a tradition which confuses scholarship with social service to the detriment of both' (p. 32). However, the moral imperative of equal opportunity and the promotion of democratic values link with a defined field of study and even a recommended pedagogy to generate not only a rationale for defence against a hostile academy, but an ethical dimension that establishes liberal adult education as a 'movement as well as a service'.

In a period when a contract culture has been established in so many areas of life, where charters enshrine individual rights, such a position may be even more difficult to sustain. Wiltshire was questioning the ability of this tradition to survive in the 1950s against the impacts of increasing access to mass higher education and the rise of qualifications in many areas of occupational activity. These trends continue to intensify, and this collection of essays is intended to reflect again on whether such work can survive into the new millennium.

The book is divided into two sections. The first section deals specifically with the general issues arising from the liberal tradition. The essays by Paterson and Lawson are general considerations of the liberal tradition by two philosophers whose work is closely associated with the values underpinning adult education. The piece by Usher and Edwards engages directly with the epistemological challenge arising from what is broadly termed 'post-modern' thinking. The very practical issues involved in maintaining university-based liberal work in the context of recent social policy are considered by Taylor, while the essay by Thompson reflects on the continuing difficulties facing forms of 'radical' intervention on behalf of 'disadvantaged/oppressed' social groups.

The second section of the collection deals with areas of work directly associated with the Nottingham department. For many years the department has worked closely with many trades unions, working with elected officials and lay members, and McIlroy's essay, which was originally written for a projected collection of essays intended as a memorial to Harold Wiltshire, uses the Nottingham experience to review the broader national scene. Alexander's essay on the role of adult education support for Zambia is a case study that illuminates this whole field of 'assistance' and support. The work of Wiltshire and others in supporting the establishment of the Open University is reflected in the essay by Keegan on the potential of distance education.

The final essay by Wallis and Allman focuses on the democratic strand in the liberal tradition and looks for ways forward both to preserve that crucial element and perhaps to radicalise it.

Finally, it should be said that all contributors to this text are primarily motivated to see the debate continue. It is hoped that the work will re-kindle discussion in areas where there has been a profound silence, and perhaps remind other sectors of our civil society — trades unions, political parties, voluntary organisations — of the debt they owe to this tradition and the continuing role it has to play.

John Wallis
March 1996

Reference

Wiltshire, H. (1956). The great tradition in university adult education. *Adult Education*, XXIX, 2. Reprinted in *The Spirit and the Form* (ed. A. Rogers, 1976). Department of Adult Education, University of Nottingham.

Education and Autonomy

R.W.K. Paterson

1. Individuals and groups

It is, I think, self-evidently true that human individuals are ontologically prior to human groups. The reality of groups derives from the reality of the individuals who compose them. The *character* of a group is of course often very different from the character of any of its individual members and usually helps to shape the characters of its members. Joining a political party or a church will tend to change the attitudes and beliefs of the individuals who join them, but this is because they will be joining up with other individuals whose attitudes and beliefs are already interrelated and interacting in a variety of complex ways which, taken together, form the distinctive character of this political party or that church. When all its members desert it, the party or church ceases to exist.

This is true of all groups, however tightly knit their members may be. If, as in a regiment or trade union, their members are closely bound by ties of loyalty and tradition, this merely means that the great majority of their present members are tied by loyalty and tradition to the whole body of members, present, past, and to come, and also to the habits of outlook, customary preferences, and styles of response which they all tend to share. These habits, preferences, and responses have to be evinced by the individuals who compose the groups in question. Otherwise they are not evinced at all, and the group no longer evinces its former character.

The same point can be made in the language of personal identity. It is individual persons who alone have a true, natural, and intrinsic identity. When we change in appearance and behaviour, as we all do, sometimes very radically and sometimes catastrophically, each of us nevertheless remains the selfsame individual person. For otherwise every change in an individual's bodily or psychological characteristics would spell the destruction of the old individual and the emergence of a completely new individual who evinces the new characteristics. And this seems to be self-evidently false. People do change, and hence we have to accept that each individual person has at least a core of identity in virtue of which he remains the selfsame individual throughout change.

It seems that only conscious selves have this kind of absolute identity. Inanimate things, such as houses or ships, indeed have an identity, but one which is merely relative and largely decided by convention. A bungalow which is converted into a two-storey house retains its old street number, but this too can change according to the decisions of the municipality. Is the RRS *Discovery*, visited by a tourist in 1995, the very same ship on which Scott sailed to the Antarctic in 1901? There is no definite and conclusive answer to this question. The vessel has been considerably altered over the years, and a tourist who wants to tread the very decks trodden by Scott and his men may go away dissatisfied. Nevertheless the official guides will claim, with much justification, that the tourist has been shown round 'Scott's *Discovery*'. Time and still greater alteration will no doubt erode this presently justified claim. However, no passage of time, and no degree of alteration, could possibly affect the identity of Robert Falcon Scott, enormously though he must have changed between his birth in 1868 and the moment forty four years later when he altogether ceased to exist.

The identity of persons is an all or nothing affair. Not so the identity of nations, tribes, institutions, families, and other groups, which even at their clearest are fuzzy round the edges and are always indefinitely variable. Is Puerto Rico part of the United States? Where does Bosnia begin and end? Is Belfast a British city or an Irish city? When two colleges merge, does each of them at this point cease to exist? Is my brother-in-law's second cousin's grandchild a member of 'my family'? The answer to all such questions is: yes, and no; for some people, but not others; perhaps at present, but not in the past, and not necessarily in the future; from some points of view and for some purposes, but not for all purposes and not from all points of view. But questions about the identity of individual persons (e.g. Is this person ringing my doorbell really who he says he is?) call for an answer which is entirely yes or no, regardless of what I or others may prefer to believe, regardless of time past or future, and regardless of our viewpoints or purposes. We may not be able to determine the answer exactly. But we can be sure that one answer is exactly true and all rival answers are wholly false.

Now it is because individuals are the true natural units of human reality that they are the true natural units of educational achievement, by reference to which educational progress has ultimately to be measured. A society which is largely made up of ignorant and narrow-minded individuals is likely to be an ignorant and narrow-minded society. A cultured and sensitive society is likely to be made up of cultured and sensitive people. Of course this is not necessarily so. Millions of ignorant people may be ruled by a comparatively small number of enlightened governors, and millions of decent people may be ruled by a self-seeking clique. In the first case, however, we should expect the governors to try to raise their ignorant subjects to something approaching their own enlightened level, and in the second case we should be surprised if the decent majority did not at last rid themselves of their selfish rulers. At any rate we should judge that both types of society are deeply unsatisfactory. And this, I suggest, is because ultimately we judge the educational level of a society, or of any group, by reference to the educational levels attained by the great majority of its individual members and because we judge that a society which denies free expression to its responsible members is by that token an unfree and irresponsible society.

2. Education and the intrinsically worthwhile

All education properly so called is the deliberate attempt to help people to appreciate what is significant and worthwhile in life and so to develop fully as persons in their own right. In the natural world, including the animal kingdom, in the worlds of art, literature, and thought, and in the world of human relations, both private and public, there is so much in which the informed intelligence can discern beauty, grace, meaning, and goodness that to leave anyone in ignorance of such things is to leave him in a kind of blindness. Certainly there is also a good deal of pain, chaos, squalor, and sheer wickedness which every educated man or woman has to see and do his or her best to remedy.

A truly educated mind has to see things in perspective, in ways which are broad and balanced, not with narrow fanaticism or mute despair. It has to measure what has value and worthwhileness against the background of everything which has disvalue and is counterworthwhile. The educated mind should strive to 'see life steadily and see it whole'.

In describing education as helping people to appreciate what is worthwhile I have in mind all those things which are *intrinsically* worthwhile. The educated person should be able to differentiate between those experiences and activities which deserve to be pursued for their own sakes, as ends in themselves, and those which are worth pursuing only because they are efficient means, that is, because they eventually lead to the appreciation of things which are worth having, doing, and enjoying in and for themselves. These two types of good, the inherent and the instrumental, are not always easy to distinguish. Often they merge, and can sometimes change places. An actress who loves acting for its own sake may take legitimate pride in the fame and fortune which her skill as an actress brings her. A man may take up carpentry simply in order to earn a living but end up as someone who takes intrinsic and continuous delight in the exercise of his craft. Equally an academic may come to tire of his academic discipline and in the end value his work only for the income and status which it still offers him. Nevertheless we can surely judge that artistic, practical, and intellectual pursuits, into which those who pursue them have to put something of their selves, are activities worth pursuing for their own sakes; whereas acquiring wealth, say, can come about by luck, the accidents of birth, or even callous deceit, and is rightly to be prized only on account of the artistic, practical, moral, or intellectual opportunities which it may open up.

In speaking of experiences and activities which are worthwhile I am of course referring to experiences and activities which are *truly* worthwhile, not just to those which are *held* to be worthwhile. If the latter concept is meaningful, then necessarily so is the former concept. We could not meaningfully hold that something had a certain characteristic unless it was actually meaningful that the thing in question could actually have the characteristic in question. All genuine beliefs are beliefs that some proposition is actually true or false. And so we must accept that some experiences and activities are more truly worthwhile than others, or that none of them is truly superior to any other, in other words that they all (miraculously) have exactly the same degree of worthwhileness.

No one sincerely believes that all experiences and activities are equivalent in value. Everyone accepts that health is better than sickness, shelter is better than homelessness, happiness is better than misery, and knowledge is better than ignorance — and also that some types of health, shelter, happiness, and knowledge are better than others. The task of education is to try to ensure that, wherever possible, people can appreciate the highest forms of knowledge and understanding not the lower, cheaper, and more trivial, that they can rise to and enjoy the most worthwhile types of human experience not the baser and more shallow, and that they can engage in the most challenging types of activity not just those which produce quicker results with less effort, skill, and involvement.

3. Autonomous individuals

Among the things in the universe which are greatly worthwhile there are many which occur naturally and without the intervention of any human agency. Natural beauties, sunlight, fresh air, animal species, trees, wild flowers and fruits — we find ourselves surrounded by many truly good things which do not owe their origin to us, although by our activities we can either preserve and improve them, or spoil, waste and destroy them. However, the domains of art, science, thought and craftsmanship, the social and public realms like government, commerce and the administration of justice, and the more private and personal spheres in which people can display qualities like kindness or constancy and can nourish relationships of trust and generosity — all these classes of deeply worthwhile things owe their existence to human agency and depend for their continuance on human beings.

I shall not attempt to discuss which of these classes of goods, the natural goods or those which are the products of human agency, is the more significant and valuable. It must suffice to point out that the latter are entirely under our control. If we disfigure our natural environment, build ugly houses, propagate error and falsehood, misgovern and act unjustly, uncharitably, or meanly, ours alone is the responsibility.

Now all human actions, whatever their social setting, are performed by individuals. A lynch mob is made up of individuals who are intent on lynching, or who want to spectate at a lynching, or who are afraid to resist the other members of the mob. There could be no companies of brutal and licentious soldiery unless there were some soldiers who were brutal and licentious and others who at least looked passively on at their brutality and licence. But whether active or passive in good or evil works, whether instigating or acquiescing in the benefits or harms produced, every individual who is aware of what is going on around him and retains some power to influence what is going on, must be judged *in that degree* to bear some responsibility for it.

Education seeks to help people to become better men and women, to foster their ability and willingness to live rightly, to think, feel and act in ways that befit their condition. Thus educators are obliged to treat all those to whom they are ministering as in some degree responsible for what they do and are.

Yet we need to distinguish between someone who *is responsible* for what he does and someone who *takes responsibility* for what he does. Very many people who are in fact in some measure responsible for some state of affairs will in various ways try to avoid shouldering any responsibility, especially when this state of affairs is one which they find it uncomfortable to contemplate. They may try to deny that the state of affairs actually has this uncomfortable moral aspect and try to argue that, properly understood, it is actually quite justifiable; or, accepting that something regrettable has indeed happened, they may try to pass the responsibility on to someone else, or on to the group or community of which they are members; or, accepting that something genuinely regrettable has come about and that they themselves played a part in bringing it about, they may plead that circumstanced as they were they had no real choice or that, given their upbringing or background, the choice which they admit having made was the only choice which such individuals, from such a background, could have been reasonably expected to make.

When we correctly judge that some particular individual has performed some action, it is obviously necessary that the action in question should have been performed by the individual in question. (If it is performed by a proxy, he himself is responsible for what the proxy does in his name and on his behalf.) In the case of actions which we judge meritorious or blameworthy it is the true author of these actions whom we judge to be truly worthy of our admiration or blame, not those who have merely been his tools or instruments. Actions do not float about in a vacuum. Some flesh-and-blood individual has to contemplate doing them, decide that on the whole they are worth doing, and then either do them himself or set or permit others to do them. Whichever means he chooses to adopt, he himself is their true author (together with all those who have given their active or passive assent or help).

Given that all moral agents are morally responsible for the actions they perform, and to some extent also for the situations in which they acquiesce, what then are *autonomous* moral agents? Let me suggest that, first and foremost, they are agents who *take responsibility* for what they are doing or leaving undone, who are willing to *acknowledge* that they are themselves the people, or are among the people, who are responsible for some given action or state of affairs. And strictly speaking I can acknowledge responsibility only if I am in fact responsible. If I am in no way responsible, my assumption of responsibility is false, just as it would be false for me to deny responsibility if I were in fact responsible.

However, there are two conditions which need to be satisfied if a person is to be correctly held responsible for what he does or permits. He has to be rational, and he has to be acting of his own free will. This is why we do not hold infants or madmen responsible and do not consider a person to be responsible if he is acting under duress. It is admittedly impossible to draw a hard-and-fast line between rationality and irrationality, and between actions done voluntarily and those done involuntarily. Nevertheless there are some people of whom we can pretty confidently say, 'He did not know what he was doing' or 'He knew very well what he was doing', and there are many occasions on which we can truly say of someone, 'He could not have helped it' or 'He could easily have helped it'.

Thus an autonomous moral agent is someone who accepts responsibility for those actions which he has performed knowingly and voluntarily. A man who acts 'heteronomously' acts from blind passion, overmastering impulse, or unthinking habit, or from docile subservience to others or fear of what others will say or think. That is, the heteronomous man does not really *act* at all. His choices are made for him — perhaps by other people, perhaps by circumstances. His character is like wax.

It does not follow that someone with a character of steel is therefore autonomous. He may be rigidly unbending merely because he lacks imagination and has a mulish obstinacy. Or he may be self-centred and narrow or the uncritical adherent of a bigoted and inward-looking creed. Although he may stand like a rock, his inflexibility is a sign, not of genuine autonomy, but merely of autarky. It proclaims the 'autos' perhaps, but not the 'nomos'. A genuinely autonomous individual is sensitive and discriminating, he has a wide range of sympathies which leave him always open to conviction, he weighs up alternatives and considers all sides of a disputed question before making up his mind.

It is in this sense that an autonomous individual thinks for himself and chooses by himself. He certainly does not do so in disregard of the interests of others or the opinions of other responsible people.

In the end what I have been saying about moral autonomy amounts, I think, to this. A morally autonomous human being is a morally good human being. His judgements are reasoned and perceptive, and he abides by what he judges and perceives; and moreover, to the extent that he is autonomous he judges and perceives clearly and correctly. He grasps what is central to a moral dilemma and acts on what he has grasped. He lives by what he understands and sees; he understands and sees what is morally relevant; and hence he has right understanding and right vision. And furthermore a morally good human being is necessarily a morally autonomous human being. This is why Kant, for example, set such store on autonomy. In this concept there is summed up the whole of man's primary obligation, which is not to be governed by accident or the intervention of others, but to live and act well by conscious design and from right motives which he willingly embraces. Hence autonomous individuals, or morally good persons, are the summit of all human achievement. They are the highest creatures, the most supremely worthwhile things, which can exist on earth.

4. Education and autonomy

Among the many tasks of education the most imperative task, by comparison with which all other educational aims are subsidiary, is the fostering of autonomy. People may be taught to read, to build, to fish, to administer, and so on, but of what avail is this if those who can now competently read, build, fish or administer can discharge these functions only like automata or serfs? Of course we all like to be nursed by skilled nurses and have our services managed by efficient managers, but we also want nurses who are committed and caring and managers who are humane and incorruptible. These two types of requirement are by no means incompatible. There is no reason why socially necessary functions should not be carried out in an ethically proper spirit. But neither are the two types of requirement necessarily mutually supportive. It may sometimes be easier, less costly and demanding, to focus exclusively on the technical efficiency with which a function is carried out and to conveniently forget that this is only one part, and the lesser part, of the function. And when technical efficiency and moral autonomy conflict, as sometimes they do, there is no doubt about which of the two we are under a paramount obligation to pursue. If we are ever likely to forget, human history, and particularly the history of the twentieth century, will savagely remind us.

The reign of the technocrat and the bureaucrat, no less than the reign of the autocrat, is the death of autonomy. No society of educated persons can ever subject itself to such zombies or half-men, or put up with being ruled by them. Nor, however, can autonomous individuals ever submit to be ruled, other than *faute de mieux*, by the will of a democracy, which in practice means the will of the majority, or their representatives, or by a transient majority of their representatives. Does it really need saying that a majority can be deeply wrong? Or that they can be misled by their political leaders? We should always hold fast to William Godwin's first principle of political justice: 'Obey *no man*'. That is: do what is right although you are ordered to do otherwise, and if you are ordered to do what is right do it *because* it is right and not because you are ordered to do it. For when we seem to do the right deed for the wrong reason, we are never really doing the right deed.

In the address given by J.M. Barrie on his installation as Chancellor of Edinburgh University, he described the idea of education as 'not so much to teach men and women what to think as how to think, not preparing them to give as little trouble in the future but sending them into it in the hope that they will give trouble'. There are echoes here of Kierkegaard's thoughts as he was sitting in the Frederiksberg Garden in Copenhagen, brooding over the fact that he had himself accomplished nothing while all around him in Europe there were so many examples of men who by their industry and ingenuity were contriving to make human life progressively easier and easier. And so, he said to himself, 'with the same humanitarian enthusiasm as the others, you must undertake to make something *harder*'. Hence, he concludes, 'I conceived it my task to *create difficulties everywhere*'.

If we are repelled by the idea that education should prepare people to know how to rock the boat, and give them the strength of character *not* to fit in to society, we need to remember that in the case of some boats it is far better that they should sink and that there are some societies into which no decent person would want to fit. We should rejoice when they collapse because only then will they be replaced by a fairer society. Indeed this is true of most social systems in Latin America, Africa, Asia, and until very recently throughout Eastern Europe. Solzhenitsyn rightly felt no obligation to fit into the social system of Soviet Russia, or Mandela to fit into the social system of apartheid. Most societies which have ever existed have been largely ruled by bullies and rogues, and if they have been fairly stable this has been because so many people have put up with being bullied and swindled day in and day out.

Of course by an autonomous individual I am postulating someone who is able to differentiate between curable injustice on the one hand, and on the other social systems into which corruption has eaten so deeply that the only remedy is to overthrow them. Every reasonable person prefers peaceful amelioration, piecemeal and gradual, and slow though it may be, to violent destruction, since violence breeds violence and tends to work, no less than corruption and injustice, as an ingrained enemy of reason.

The concept of autonomy as I have been outlining it is obviously the concept of an ideal. It may well be objected that a society made up of morally perfect men and women will of course need no governors set over them, but when has such a society ever existed and how can it ever be brought about? To this objection there is an obvious answer. Unless we have in mind clear goals to pursue, clear objectives to which we should be heading, we cannot meaningfully set one foot before another, because we have no idea in which direction we ought to travel. Then we shall in effect *drift*, now to the left, then to the right, sometimes backwards, sometimes forwards, completely out of navigational control. We must at least have short-term objectives, but unless these are to be immediately abandoned on attainment, short-term objectives have to be clearly perceived as stages towards a destination we are aiming at in the long term, perhaps even long after everyone who is now alive. Such remote goals, viewed as ideals, may seem hopelessly theoretical. But in fact they are eminently practical, since they help us to realise where we are, whither we are now going, and what progress we have actually made. Without ideals, individuals and societies are practically *lost*.

Educators, above all, cannot afford to suffer from myopia. Even their simplest efforts cannot bear fruit within weeks or months. The outcome of their best and highest efforts will not be visible for years, possibly many years, and perhaps generations — despite the 'promises' of politicians, who can seldom see further than four or five years ahead. Politicians, perhaps especially democratic politicians, are the natural enemies of educators, or of anyone whose thoughts stretch beyond the next election. It is in the teeth of politicians that educators, in season and out of season, have to stick to their appointed task.

5. Education and values

Because the supreme task of education is to foster autonomy, that is, to nourish people's capacity to make independent judgements which are reasoned and perceptive, educators themselves cannot avoid making judgements of value. It is not enough for them to endorse those values which happen to be socially acceptable or 'politically correct'. In the long run some of these values may come to be shown to have been unacceptable and incorrect, even at the times and in the places where they have been transiently adopted and regarded as sacrosanct. Like those whom they are striving to educate, all teachers have to begin by trying to clear their minds of cant, thinking critically and therefore undogmatically about disputed questions, and attempting to see clearly the issues which lie before them without prejudice or prepossession.

It is because people are and always will be far from morally and intellectually perfect that there is and always will be a need for education. We are all at best struggling (though many of us are not even trying to struggle) to get a better view of life and build a self which conforms to this better view rather than to the distorting perspective shown within our tunnel vision. Those who have managed to gain somewhat wider glimpses of the whole picture have a duty to share what they have learned with others who are still trying to peer over the edge, and perhaps above all to try to convince people whose eyes remain tightly shut that if they will only take the trouble to look they will find that their efforts are well rewarded. I am of course not suggesting that the human race is divided into three classes — those who are educated, those who want to become educated, and those who do not want any part of it. These are rather three ingredients which are to some extent present in all of us, although, it must be said, in more marked proportion in some of us than in others. But at least I can confidently assert that all those individuals who are in some measure educationally advantaged have a clear duty to share their advantages, wherever possible, with their fellow human beings who for one reason or another have been denied them.

It may be asked: how can anyone be sure that one type of experience or activity is educationally preferable to another? One answer is that, while no one can be absolutely *sure*, someone who is well acquainted with both types of experience, or has engaged meaningfully in both types of activity, is better placed to make judgements about their comparative value than someone who has direct knowledge of one of them only. He will then, I suggest, tend to regard studies which focus on matters central to the human condition as more worthwhile than those which deal only with topics which are peripheral; he will give priority to forms of activity which are relatively complex and challenging, which really stretch everyone who participates in them, over forms of activity which are fairly simple and undemanding, and which students can simply coast through; and he will reasonably give preference to those kinds of knowledge which shed light on the whole of the rest of human knowledge, rather than those which are relatively self-contained and which have merely parochial or temporary significance. Such judgements are difficult and will always be contentious. But in constructing curricula, *some* differences have to be made and *some* things have to be given priority. Even if a completely personal curriculum were to be devised for a single student, to meet his unique educational needs, those responsible would still need to answer the question: what kinds of experience and activity do we judge will in the end be educationally best for this individual person to encounter and grapple with? Indeed this question needs to be answered even if the student is wholly responsible for his own education. Unless he judges that everything is exactly equal in value for all his educational needs — a judgement he would not dream of making about health, housing, personal relationships, or financial matters, for example — he is forced to discriminate, to the best of his ability, between what is more educationally worthwhile and what is less educationally worthwhile.

It might seem that the difficulties involved in making the value judgements which we need to make for education in general are particularly acute when we have to make those specifically *moral* judgements without which no attempt to foster character development, no attempt to develop moral autonomy, can even begin. If we find it hard to decide whether it is more important for a history student to learn about nineteenth century Britain or about the Peloponnesian War, or for a drama student to become familiar with Elizabethan stagecraft or with the revolutionary theatre of Brecht, how much harder it may seem to equip students, and ourselves, so that we can respond meaningfully to the dilemmas by which we are directly confronted when we are required to face questions about war and peace, liberty and restraint, justice and generosity, in addition to the myriad issues which we all have to resolve in our private lives and relationships.

However, part of the answer has I think just been given. There are moral issues which we *have* to strive to resolve, however daunting they may be. We cannot just hang about, waiting for the solutions to drop from a cloud. If we sit on the fence, we are thereby acquiescing in the triumph of the cause that is winning on one or the other side of the fence. If we postpone our decision, there will come a time when we can postpone it no longer. Sooner or later we have to make up our minds, at least provisionally.

But we are not in fact left altogether without resources by means of which we can try to settle which of the possible answers is more reasonable than others on the different sides of a moral question. Sometimes empirically discoverable facts can make a contribution. Who struck the first blow, or made the first openly threatening gesture? What degree of sentience, including susceptibility to pain, can be attributed to a normal five-months old foetus? Does a fox in fact suffer very acute distress while being hunted? Reliable answers to such obviously empirical questions are often far from easy to establish with even a fair measure of probability. But there is no doubt that our moral attitudes towards fox-hunting, abortion, cases of physical conflict, and so on, are often profoundly (and rightly) influenced by what we take to be some of the essential facts of the matter. And further empirical research can always help us to establish more of these relevant facts more securely.

Empirical research can also help us to predict more confidently the probable consequences of our different choices. Suppose we intervene in, or stand aside from, some physical conflict. Will this reduce the scale of the conflict, or tend to exacerbate it? Will we ourselves, and those dependent on us, be thereby safer or less safe? Do legal restrictions on abortion tend to encourage the spread of more dangerous 'backstreet abortions'? What might be the effect of a ban on fox-hunting on the overall welfare of the human and animal population (including the fox population) of the countryside? Once again it is impossible to forecast the consequences of our choices with any very high degree of exactitude. But once again we have to make our best efforts to predict the *most probable* consequences, with the help of historical, scientific, sociological, and other methods of empirical inquiry, since it is obviously better to know where our policies are on the whole likely to lead than to remain in total ignorance.

We can also use analogies as a means of illuminating moral issues. Is unauthorised use of the firm's telephone for private calls analogous to other ways of helping oneself to the firm's property, that is, does it constitute a kind of theft? Or is it a very minor type of dishonesty, more like leaving the office a few minutes before our scheduled time? Obviously the size of a delinquency can transform our perception of its nature. And obviously we can, and often do, argue about the relevance of analogies and cases offered as moral parallels. Many people would resist comparisons of abortion with infanticide, for example, and others would deny the validity of expressions like 'acute distress' when applied to creatures like foxes. Nevertheless analogical reasoning does often help us to see moral similarities between those cases where we are in little doubt and those cases where we experience considerable doubt, as when people who have no doubt about the wrongness of racial discrimination, but who are highly sceptical about the claimed wrongness of discrimination on grounds of sex, can come to see that there are legitimate parallels between these two types of discrimination. It is by the fruitful use of analogies that much moral education takes place.

Another asset on which our moral understanding can draw is our ability to recognise specious arguments. The man who is unfaithful to his wife may tell himself, 'Everyone does it these days'. The shop assistant who regularly pilfers may tell herself, 'They underpay me anyway'. The man who falsifies his tax returns may tell himself, 'The Inland Revenue don't really expect me to tell the whole truth and nothing but the truth'. They may try to make it sound as if wrong becomes right when it is widespread, as if low wages always justify theft, and as if people's suspicions of liars are in themselves a justification for lying. The reasons they adduce could at most be somewhat extenuating factors, since it is obviously worse to steal from your employers if you are being fairly paid than if you are being underpaid by them, but there is a huge difference, which we can all easily understand, between factors which extenuate and factors which totally exculpate. The fact, if it is a fact, that a group of people suspects that I might lie to them, for example, in no way tends to justify any lies which I may then deliberately proceed to tell them.

There are, then, modes of reasoning which we can employ when we are trying to clarify the validity of our moral judgements; they are all available to anyone who is trying to develop his moral autonomy, his capacity to think for himself about the differences between right and wrong; and they are available to educators who are trying to foster the development of autonomy. However, *reasoning* about moral questions, on its own, is not enough. All thinking needs to be supplied with *data* into which the reasoning process can get its teeth. Thus moral reasoning has to revolve around the data which make up the ultimate subject-matter of our moral lives. In the end we have to be able to *see*, as it were, that certain states of affairs are intrinsically desirable or undesirable, that they are the kinds of thing we ought to strive to bring about or to prevent, and that the actions which intentionally bring them about or prevent them are therefore actions which can be correctly judged to be morally right or wrong actions.

Perceiving the intrinsic desirability or undesirability of something is no doubt often difficult, but not nearly as difficult as we are sometimes led to believe. Our capacities for *feeling* have to be allowed to operate in unrestricted ways. Almost everyone who contemplates the deliberate breaking of a promise, say, or the suffering of intense pain, will react with feelings of abhorrence or pity. Almost everyone accepts that it is wrong to break promises and bad to suffer pain. When we fail to feel abhorrence and pity, this is nearly always because we are failing to focus attentively on the breach of faith or the pain involved, and are instead focusing on the circumstances (often indeed morally relevant) by which they are preceded, accompanied, or followed, and which can blur our appreciation of the intrinsic wrongness of the breach of faith and the horridness of the pain. Obviously a promise extracted under duress may be broken without our feeling abhorrence, and we may feel relief when someone's temporarily intense pain is accepted because it is a necessary means towards his avoiding still greater pain in the future. We have to judge the whole situation. But the whole situation is composed of its elements, each of which needs to be separately assessed and its precise role identified, if we are to arrive at a correct assessment of the situation as a whole. If we slip up, we could find ourselves taking a more casual attitude towards the making and keeping of promises in general or tolerating people's pain in circumstances where there is no real need for them to suffer it.

By far the most effective way of developing sensitive and sound feeling responses is to gain direct personal knowledge of the situations to which such responses are appropriate. No one who has himself encountered unfair treatment, or lived through periods of deep wretchedness, is likely to doubt that these are great evils. However, educators can hardly expose themselves and their students to the entire range of happy and painful experiences, of generous and brutal actions, by which human life is filled and which solicit our moral judgments. Most of what we learn we learn at second hand, from the experiences of others. Our powers of *imagination* therefore need to be stretched and our capacities for *sympathy* sharpened. In our efforts to do this we can turn to didactic studies like psychology and sociology, but it is surely by looking at very many concrete examples of heroism and selfishness, as we find them in history and biography and still more vividly through their artistic representations in literature, drama, and film, that our hearts can be more directly stirred and our imaginative sympathy kindled.

There is no limit to moral development, and so there is no end to the quest for autonomy. It can not only be nourished in the young, but also continuously strengthened and enhanced in those of maturer years, who can say with Tennyson's Ulysses:

> I will drink life to the lees:
> All times I have enjoyed greatly,
> Have suffered greatly, both with those that loved me
> And alone....
> Life piled on life
> Were all too little, and of one to me
> Little remains: but every hour is saved
> From that eternal silence, something more,
> A bringer of new things.

And with Ulysses every human being in later life can reaffirm his resolve to go on:

> Though much is taken, much abides; and though
> We are not now that strength which in old days
> Moved earth and heaven; that which we are, we are;
> One equal temper of heroic hearts,
> Made weak by time and fate but strong in will
> To strive, to seek, to find, and not to yield.

From Citizen to Self

Political and Ethical Foundations of Liberal Adult Education

Kenneth Lawson

This chapter is based upon the assumption that adult education is not free-standing and can only be studied within a broader cultural context which provides its values. In an earlier essay (Lawson, 1985), I explored connections between 'deontological' or 'rights-based' liberalism and liberal adult education, but a broader view is necessary in order to produce a more accurate picture. Other dimensions within the liberal tradition will be drawn upon because they, too, correlate with theory and practice in adult education.

Neither 'liberalism' nor 'liberal adult education' are simple concepts and they are not static. It is because they change, that the idea of a 'tradition' is introduced. It suggests dynamism in response to changing circumstances.

Alasdair MacIntyre (1988) has suggested that the original liberal project was seen by many as an attempt to escape from the contingency of tradition by 'appealing to genuinely tradition-independent norms'. The new norms were thought to be universal whereas they constituted a particular vision of an ideal political system. What emerged was another tradition with its own values which became definitive of and normative within the tradition. The new vision was *meant* to be *liberating* but it was also *constraining*, thus creating inherent tensions.

The subsequent history of liberalism might be seen in part as a series of attempts to remove the tension by slackening the normative requirements, but it will be argued that this is not an achievable goal. By reducing the number of defining characteristics, the tradition becomes less determinate, more ambiguous, and in the end dissolves. To be a tradition at all, recognisable limits are essential, although it does not follow that change is impossible. New norms may be introduced but these can change the tradition in ways that make it incompatible with its earlier manifestations. It ceases to be recognisable as the same tradition.

This seems to be happening, or to have happened already and it is now difficult to be precise about what is meant by 'liberalism' in either political or educational terms. It becomes necessary therefore to identify different strands and to attempt some form of classification. This will be done selectively within the confines of a single essay and no attempt is made to present a potted history. The selections are meant to be illustrative only, and where they are linked, the connections are in logical rather than in temporal sequence, even though this might make the argument somewhat disjointed. The author can see a pattern and it is hoped that readers will do so, too.

What might we mean by 'liberalism'?

In *A Matter of Principle*, Ronald Dworkin (1986: 181, 183) explores the hypothesis put forward by sceptics that politically speaking, 'there is no such thing as liberalism although his project suggests that there is'. We are in a similar position.

Dworkin continues, '... before the Vietnam war, politicians who called themselves "liberals" held certain *positions* that could be identified as a group. Liberals were for greater economic equality, for internationalism, for freedom of speech, for greater equality between races, for procedural protection of accused criminals ... and for an aggressive use of central government power to achieve these goals.'

This last point might seem strange to those who regard *minimal* government as a liberal ideal. Minimal government is also a mark of modern conservatism, and it is this kind of ambiguity in practice which makes liberalism difficult to identify. But it clearly is not a prerogative of any one political party and in that sense it is politically neutral. Dworkin's list of 'causes' is given unity by a number of common *principles* which include 'equality', 'freedom' and 'justice', although he himself argues that 'the nerve of liberalism' is 'a certain concept of equality'.

Thomas Nagel (1982: 191) suggests that liberalism is '...the conjunction of two ideals ... the first of which is individual liberty' and the second is a 'democratic society controlled by its citizens'. For him, liberty is a prime value and democracy is merely a mechanism which makes liberty possible. It does not necessarily follow that democracy entails minimal government and Nagel makes a minimalist conclusion dependent upon his particular definition of liberty. This he *defines* as '...freedom from government interference with privacy, personal life and the exercise of individual inclinations'. Other definitions are possible.

J.S. Mill (1859 and 1962: 135) made a similar point in his *Essay on Liberty* although he allowed governments to intervene in private life in certain circumstances. Mill actually defines very narrowly the area of 'private space' and he makes his individuals sovereign only over their 'own body and mind' and an individual in his theory should *always* be prevented from doing harm to others. His utilitarianism also takes him beyond this point, and despite saying that no one should be forced to act for their *own* good, he claimed that '...there are many positive acts for the benefit of others which [an individual] may rightfully be *compelled* to perform' (1859 and 1962: 136).

Mill's stance, in effect, makes the good of others at least as important as a concern for privacy and self-interest and by holding these two points in a finely balanced tension, he can say, without contradiction, that we may be *required* to perform 'acts of beneficence' (1859 and 1962: 131).

This brings us back to Dworkin's claim about the importance of 'equality' which is implicit in Mill's argument about the good of others and the obligation to be beneficent. Nagel (1982: 191) also introduces the idea of equality when he says that, in order to make his other principles operative, it is necessary that there should be no 'excessive ... inequalities of political and economic power and social position'.

We can see in this discussion how various principles inter-relate in a systematic way and in doing so become normative, by definition. Moreover, none of the principles are brought in from other systems. They are already *liberal* principles and liberal values and their justification is implicit within the system. They are already justified because they *are* liberal principles; they are constitutive of liberalism. They provide the basis for its rules, define the 'game' as it has evolved, and have no force beyond it.

This brings out a further point, namely that the liberal vision of politics is rule-based. It is a rational form of politics in the sense that it relates ideas in a logical sequence. Its inherent rationality is the reference point for guiding and judging action. Mill (1859 and 1962: 136) reinforces this view when he says that, '... liberty as a principle has no application to any state of things anterior to the time when mankind has become capable of being improved by free and equal *discussion*. Until that time, there is nothing but implicit obedience...'.

This emphasis on discussion as a necessary condition for achieving liberty amounts to an implicit injunction on the use of force for that end, although that is not Mill's purpose. His stress on discussion arises from a belief that '*individuality*' is expressible only through an ability 'to form opinions' and 'to express them without reserve' (1859 and 1962: 184). Individuality is therefore being, defined in terms of the ability to discuss in order that 'liberty' may then be defined as 'freedom to discuss.' Both 'liberty' and 'discussion' help to define 'individuality' which would otherwise have no place in Mill's vocabulary. For him, 'liberty' cannot be defined any other way. Not even the *nature* of our opinion counts. It is sufficient that we have opinions of *some* kind and can express them.

We might summarise this brief discussion in the following terms:

i)   Liberalism represents a strongly moral approach to politics. Dworkin's list of 'causes' consists of goals which *ought* to be realised. They are not simply 'causes' which it would be politically *expedient*, although they might additionally have utilitarian purpose.

ii)   The causes cited are 'worthy' because they embody principles such as 'freedom' and 'equality' which are accepted as good justificatory reasons for taking action. These principles are simultaneously *concepts* and goals.

iii) There is a rational approach to politics based upon a rationality of seeking definable 'goods' rather than a naked struggle for power as an end. The goal is to control and define power, but by rational means as a normative principle.

iv)   The concept of individuality is primary for several reasons:
      a) individuals provide the starting point of all thought and action.
      b) they are also deemed to be the end point or purpose of action.

v)   There is concern not only for self-interest but also the interests and welfare of others. There is a concern for responsibilities and duties, as well as rights.

Nevertheless this represents only one strand of liberalism within the broader tradition, because it emphasises the welfare of others, and is concerned with duties as well as rights. We might designate it by using Mill's own term, 'beneficence' to describe it as 'beneficent liberalism'; it might equally be called 'classical liberalism'.

We turn now to a review of some of the historical roots of this strand before considering others within the tradition. In doing so, I wish to draw particular attention to two major developments. The first is the changing perception of the nature of individuality and its role in political thought. The second, which is a consequence of the first, is the shift away from the idea of a public good towards the idea of private good. A third might be added as a gloss on each of these, and that is the narrowing of definitions of social relationships which weakens the values of 'community' implicit in the 'classical' strand.

Historical roots

We begin conventionally with Athenian democracy as it appeared towards the end of the fifth century B.C. The account given is based substantially on a relatively new study by Cynthia Farrar (1989), who stresses the importance of concrete political issues as determinants of political theory.

Athenian democracy developed in a situation in which States were already established and what we would call problems of 'international relations' were a cause for concern. Fear of domination by another State was the most urgent problem and one especially important aspect was the fear of slavery, which conquest would bring if Athens lost her sovereignty. This is an especially important point because out of it developed the Athenian concept of negative freedom. It was simply 'freedom from slavery', and this concept had a profound effect upon Athenian thought and practice concerning internal government of the City State.

A strong government was obviously essential in order to maintain this freedom and effective control of social order was an important prerequisite for this end. The fear of slavery, that is to say, a loss of freedom in a very practical sense, provided a social bond which united private interests with the public interest. Individual freedom in the sense in which it was then understood, was dependent upon State sovereignty which, in turn, was recognised as being dependent upon the support of its citizens. This sense of mutual support was thus expressed in the institution of democratic government as an enabling mechanism, not a 'good', except to the extent that it fulfils a utilitarian purpose in securing commitment to political decisions. In fact, by the time of Plato, who was an anti-democrat, the idea of democracy was in disrepute.

On the back, as it were, of this very practical view of democracy a total view of social and political life was developing. From an internal point of view, 'the Athenians', as Farrar (1989: 7) puts it, 'did not construe the good to be secured politically in terms of direct material advantage. Political life expressed a shared, ordered self-under-standing, not a mere struggle for power'. These were quite sophis-ticated political ideals which were normative for an Athenian for whom '... political status, the status of the citizen both marked and shaped man's identification with those aspects of human nature that made possible a reconciliation of personal aims and social order.' This, Farrar (1989: 1) regards as a 'striking vision' of political principles. We may also see it as introducing the moral element into political life. Good citizenship became a moral imperative accepted voluntarily, but the idea of voluntarism depended in turn upon the ideal of citizens as 'autonomoi'; they had to be autonomous choosers in order to be deemed responsible for actions. Thus principle became interwoven with principle and what began as a limited concept of freedom devel-oped into a set of ideas fundamental to the Athenian system. Abstract ideas and theory became a part of politics and social life in 'a dynamic synthesis of the concrete and the reflective'. But the process of devel-opment was piecemeal and as Farrar wryly comments, 'democracy was cobbled together' (1989: 1). It did not arrive as a ready-made dream but as a result of communal effort and, as H.D.F. Kitto (1964: 11) expresses it, '... the city-state was the means by which the Greeks consciously strove to make life, both of the community and of the individual, more excellent than it was before.' What began as '... a local association for common security, became the focus of man's moral, intellectual, aesthetic, social and practical life, developing and enriching these in a way in which no form of society had done before or has done since.'

It must of course be recognised that the citizens of Athens did not comprise the whole of its population because they were supported by a sub-stratum of slaves and foreigners who had no part in political life. Citizenship was attained by birth and as G.H.Sabine (1949: 19) puts it, 'what citizenship entitled a man to was "*membership*"' and this is a point which cannot be too heavily stressed when we look at the roots of modern liberalism. The concepts of individuality and autonomy were important but they were given expression in and through the sense of *membership* and it will be argued below that in more recent liberal thought, the emphasis has shifted excessively in favour of a socially disembodied form of individuality. We might, for want of a better term, call this 'post-modern' liberalism, or if preferred, we can use the clumsy term 'deontological liberalism'. It still falls within the same tradition but in many ways it is the opposite of Mill's 'beneficent' liberalism, which is more firmly rooted in classical thought. But new forms are a response to changing historical situations, and this should not surprise us if it is accepted that the liberal tradition is not a neutral philosophical tradition but one firmly rooted in practice.

Changing rationalities

In Athenian thought and in the writings of Mill we noted the stress placed upon the role of discussion as the basis of political life. This, when coupled with the idea of reflection, highlights the importance of 'reason' in liberal, democratic tradition. It was present at the beginning and has since become implicit as a constitutive element.

Thought and practice would cease to be liberal if reason was denied, because the liberal conception of mankind portrays men and women as rational beings, self-aware and articulate. Reason is made a precondition for 'autonomy'.

Philosophers such as Descartes (1637 and 1913) suggest that the capacity to think rationally is in some way 'natural' or innate, whereas the passage already quoted from Mill implies that the capacity developed historically. MacIntyre (1988) seems to share Mill's view when he says that intellectual enquiry, which pre-supposes rational thought, 'is part of the elaboration of a mode of social and moral life'. On this view 'rationality' does not depend upon abstract universal principles, it is something that is shared by those within a tradition within which particular rationalities evolved.

If this view is correct (and it is difficult to establish how any intellectual tradition can be established beyond all tradition, because we are speaking of human invention), the way is then open to the possibility of a multiplicity of rationalities and this, indeed, is the thrust of MacIntyre's argument.

There is a difficulty here, which MacIntyre (1988) admits, with the idea of logic as universal and he accepts areas of agreement in *some* standards for the regulation of argument. Nevertheless, within the liberal tradition there can be discerned differing views on what are acceptable as good reasons put forward in justification of particular actions and policies. Such variability is implied by the idea of a liberal tradition as distinct from a single liberal doctrine, because the latter would be unnecessarily restrictive and in itself a denial of liberalism. 'Tradition' both allows and requires recognition of difference, otherwise it ceases to be 'tradition' and this too is illustrative of tensions within liberalism because recognition of difference and plurality also becomes constitutive. The idea echoes Rousseau's famous call that we must 'force men to be free' and the paradox arises wherever 'freedom', however defined, becomes constitutive or normative for a tradition of thought.

I am aware of ambiguity in running together terms such as 'reason', 'rationality' and 'reflection', but for our present purpose these seem to be sufficiently cognate. We are already familiar with the idea of different forms of reasoning in the two examples 'inductive' and 'deductive' and Toulmin (1961) has explored different forms of reasoning in his book *Reason in Ethics*. The idea is also implicit in Wittgenstein's (1958) metaphor of 'language games' in which the 'logic' of a move and hence the meaning of words is definable only within a particular game or discourse.

One form of discourse is present in Athenian political thought and practice. For the Athenian citizen it was rational to identify and define personal goals in the light of the shared aim of preserving the independence and sovereignty of Athens. That a particular action was conducive to this end was a good and sufficient reason for recommending and taking that action. Such reasoning defined their political rationality.

Within this framework an idea such as 'autonomy' seemed *initially* to be pragmatically useful as a means of securing commitment although, as we have observed, there were constraints on what would be deemed 'good' or rational to choose. Choices had to be consistent with the value system as a whole and it is this sense of inter-relatedness which makes it 'rational' within the root sense of that word, which is 'ratio' as 'the relationship of one thing to another'.

A different approach is evident in two other examples that have been used, namely Mill and Nagel. In his Essay, Mill (1859 and 1962: 126, 205) uncompromisingly spells out his project as being concerned with 'the nature and limits of the power which can be legitimately exercised by society over the individual'. The obverse of this is to define 'the rightful limit to the sovereignty of the individual'. Nagel (1982) expresses himself differently but he and Mill are concerned with the same issues, namely:

i)   the rights of individuals and the definition of their private space;

ii)   the promotion of a society which serves the needs of individuals.

Here the implied rationality is not expressed in terms of defending the State by concerted effort. The first concern is to protect individual interests and this is the prime function of government. It is rational to do whatever is most conducive to *this* end. The first question must always be 'what promotes individual interests?' but, as Nagel (1982) observes, it is difficult to pursue the private and the public good simultaneously, hence Mill's claim that privacy may be invaded to do good to others. The political problem is to achieve some kind of unstable equilibrium in which the instability is the inevitable result of trying to define societal goals in terms of the sum of individual goods. There is no *independently defined public good* and this is why Mill has to introduce the idea of 'utility' as something to be maximised. We end up with a 'utilitarian' rationality which judges the validity of action on the basis of what produces the greatest total good. An action which achieves this is a rational action. It is Mill's solution to Nagel's problem, and it maintains the principle of 'beneficence.'

In John Locke (1698 and 1956), writing in the seventeenth century, a very different strand in the liberal tradition begins. Superficially he is dealing with the same issues as Mill, in that he too is concerned with protecting the sovereignty of individuals. But two differences stand out. Locke is much more specific in his target, which is the containment of absolute monarchy, and Locke's individual is very differently conceived.

Starting from a natural law position he postulates an individual as having a natural law right to life and also rights to property or possessions, including the property of one's own body. The defence of property is the key to his rationality. Individuals, says Locke (1690 and 1956: 5), are 'in a state of perfect freedom to order their actions and dispose of their possessions and persons as they think fit within the bounds of nature, without asking leave'. Preservation of this freedom provides the foundation for a political platform to which his theory is directed.

His emphasis is not however on 'reason' and 'discussion' *per se*. He is concerned with a very much more circumscribed framework of rights enforcing law. The State, for Locke, becomes a regulator of contractual relationships between individuals and between individuals and the

State. His rationality is procedural in the sense of being concerned with the application of rules, and the starting point is always of the form 'what rules govern this kind of case?' 'What are the procedures to be followed?'

Democracy is the preferred form of government, not in order to secure loyalty and commitment as in Athens, but as a mechanism for the diffusion of power. Locke is therefore consistent in his avowed aim of weakening, not strengthening government. In doing so, he allows individuals to get on with their own business governed by legal rather than moral obligation. Nevertheless, his individuals are members of a body politic (Locke, 1698 and 1956: 87), as C.B.MacPherson (1962) puts it, 'their individualism is necessarily collectivism' and yet again we find a tension between opposing poles as a feature of the liberal tradition. On the one hand individuals are regarded as having freedoms of various kinds but always within a constraining framework which guarantees those freedoms.

In more recent years, Locke has been reformulated in the deontological liberalism of Rawls (1972) and Nozick (1982) each of whom begins with the idea of 'radically situated' individuals in the sense that as Cartesian selves, they are rooted only in their own self-consciousness. Their initial existence owes nothing to society.

Rawls' purpose is to design a universally valid rational society, that is to say, a model which *any* rational person would design. Such a society by definition would be free from ideology and it would be self-evidently acceptable by consent. Such acceptance would represent a perfect example of free choice, unfettered by any contingencies.

In order to achieve this state of affairs, Rawls relies upon a theoretical abstraction called, 'the veil of ignorance', behind which his individuals can deliberate free from any awareness of their own interests or other contingencies which might distort their thinking. What they produce in these circumstances would be legitimated in two ways:

i)   the result would be an act of free choice;

ii)   such a choice would be rational.

What emerges, and of course it is Rawls (1972: 124) who produces it — and *he* is *not* behind a veil of ignorance, is a society based on 'justice', but it is a 'distributive' concept of justice based upon the principle of greatest equal liberty and the principle of equal opportunity. It is a concept of justice uniquely adapted to be a regulatory principle for the distribution of welfare and economic goods.

Unlike the Athenians who construed their goals politically, Rawlsian individuals construe their goals and goods economically in a market. The rationality involved is a market rationality which in principle balances marginal utilities between competing individuals. A further refinement is the incorporation of a 'rights ethic' supported by a legal framework of rights defining, and rights protecting, procedures. There are no over-riding public 'goods' beyond such procedures and the prime shared value is the right to choose.

An individual's right to the possession of goods (property in Locke's terminology) is justified by Nozick (1974: 151) in an 'entitlement theory' which states that a given distribution is 'just' '... if everyone is entitled to the holdings they possess' and the entitlement is defined in terms of the manner in which possessions are acquired, and this means that the appropriate legal regulatory procedures should have been followed.

This is all very clearly a set of views which are highly consistent with free market economics and every principle expressed by Rawls and Nozick is presupposed or implied within various branches of the liberal tradition. The authors are not neutral, they are already liberals, committed to a number of values before they start. Their alleged rational choices made behind the veil of ignorance are not neutrally made. They are the choices of already committed liberals in a particular historical context and the problems which they are addressing are problems which liberals would recognise as problems.

What is important from our present point of view, is the direction in which the liberal tradition has moved? It is no longer 'beneficent' in Mill's sense, nor corporate in the Athenian sense of contributing to a good society. It envisages instead a society which has tried to reduce its shared values to legal frameworks and regulatory procedures.

What is significant in this kind of theorising is the shift in emphasis away from individuals as members of society to which they make a positive contribution. This shift involves a demoting of the idea of public good in favour of private goods as the overriding priority. The private domain is given higher moral status simply because, within it, 'goods' are defined and chosen by individuals. But what appears as a moral claim is also a political claim to support the idea of minimal government. This is not an end in itself, however, it is a move towards the development of individualism.

Attempts have been made to root the new moral position entirely within a single principle, and an example is Ayn Rand, an American writer whose ideas are scattered in her novels and essays. Her general position is discussed in two articles, one by Nozick (1982: 231) and one by Douglas Den Vyl and Douglas Rasmussen (1982:232-269). The arguments are complex but they seem to be reducible to the following propositions which attempt to make 'life' the ultimate and irreducible value:

i)   life is an ultimate end, an end in itself for any living thing;

ii)   to be a living thing, and not to be a living thing of a particular kind, is impossible;

iii)   the particular kind of living thing an entity is determines what one must mean when talking of life with respect to a given entity;

iv)   thus life as the kind of thing it is, is the ultimate value for each living thing (Den Vyl and Rasmussen, 1982: 257).

Points i) and iv) are value judgements while ii) and iii) are truisms. To have an 'end' presupposes that only sentient living things are included in i), while iv) implies that the kind of life referred to is both sentient and rational and can, therefore, rank order its values, or as Nozick (1974: 207) puts it, can have 'a rational preference pattern'. Therefore we are talking about human beings as persons and Nozick concludes that '*life as a rational* person is a value to the person whose life it is'.

Den Vyl and Rasmussen (1982: 250) conclude that being rational entails the ability to formulate and use concepts, by which they mean 'acting in accordance with conceptual judgements' to sustain one's own existence. 'Thus a precondition for living the life of a rational animal is that within *any* given context one must be *free from interference* upon acting according to one's judgement' (my italics).

A further point is made by Rand herself who, in arguing that the achievement of a happy existence is a person's highest aim, writes that

> Happiness is that state of consciousness which proceeds from the achievement of one's values. If a man values productive work, his happiness is the means of his success in the service of his life. But if a man values ... mindless kicks ... *his* alleged happiness is the measure of his success in the service of his own destruction ... and when one experiences the kind of pure happiness that is an end in itself — the kind that makes one think: 'This is worth living for' — what one is greeting and affirming in emotional terms is the meta-physical fact that *life* is an end in itself.
>
> Quoted Den Vyl and Rasmussen (1982: 262).

A number of comments might be made about this kind of argument:

i)   it makes personal judgement and freedom to act upon it an implied right because our humanity depends upon it;

ii) despite the affirmation of 'rationality', the ultimate achievement for a human being (despite our freedom to destroy ourselves if we choose), is ultimately a psychological sense of happiness or 'joy';

iii) nevertheless, striving to achieve this sense of joy is the only rational thing for a human being to do. The final goal itself is non-rational as it must be if it has no purpose beyond itself.

The significance of all this for our present purposes is to illustrate but one attempt to move the liberal tradition in the direction of individualism. The goal is no longer the good society, or democratic government or any other political goal. The final achievement is located in individuals themselves. It need not follow that they are excluded from acting, say, as 'citizens' if that makes them happy, but they need not do so. Moreover, the only moral constraint to be imposed is that of Mill's, which requires such individual to have freedom to act on his or her own judgement. By implication this means freedom in all respects except those cases in which an action impedes that of another person. We have not quite arrived at anarchy but we appear to be very close to it. We should also note the similarity between the Randian and the Rawlsian argument in that each stresses the importance of personal preferences and that both are products of the early 1970s.

In terms of changing rationalities within the liberal tradition, we may describe the new rationality in terms of seeking personal satisfaction. There can still be a place for corporate action and individual acts of self-sacrifice, but the justification for them is in the 'joy' which they give to the actor.

Alasdair MacIntyre (1988: 338) expresses the new mood in the following terms:

> ... in the liberal public realm individuals understand each other and themselves as each possessing his or her own ordered schedule of preferences ... Each individual therefore, in contemplating prospective action, has first to ask ...'What are my wants?' The answers ... provide the initial premise for the practical reasoning of such individuals expressed as an utterance of the form, 'I want it to be the case that such and such' or of some closely cognate form.

Preference individualism, as we might now call it, has replaced 'I ought ...' with 'I want' and this is a very different ethical claim.

The new claim in its barest form carries no implication of relationships, of citizenship or membership of society. Such things are now mechanisms which might be useful but they are not of inherent value.

However, although the emphasis might now be more extreme, there are still echoes of John Locke, and it is this kind of connection which enables us to place our various examples within the same tradition.

One of the issues now raised is how each individual arrives at a sense of his or her identity. The new injunction is akin to that of Ibsen's character whose cry is 'to thine own self be true', which in modern terms is expressed by the concept of 'authenticity.' But how do we arrive at it? What does it consist of?

The problem of authenticity

In Rawlsian terms, we have been left with a very thin definition of the self which consists of little more than the 'I' which thinks or the Kantian centre of consciousness and 'will.' If our individual is unfettered by contingency where does one begin when defining authenticity?

Charles Taylor (1992: 33) has suggested that a menu of languages is a pre-requisite and these are 'not only the words we speak but also other modes of expression in terms of which we define ourselves.' This suggestion immediately brings in a social frame of reference because, by definition, a language is a medium of communication. Individuals may attempt to modify existing languages but if they are too novel communication breaks down.

The danger of this happening has been discussed by Lyotard (1979) as one of our modern (or postmodern?) dilemmas. The search for novelty, in his view, has produced a plurality of modes of expression which are the languages of particular groups. This he suggests leads to the destruction of generally available languages which are an important social bond. The idea of a 'culture' is expressible in terms of such bonds, but we are, he claims, moving towards a culture of sub-cultures. Individuals and members of sub-groups are encouraged to be self-defining but 'each of us knows that our self does not amount to much.' Despite a narrow view of 'self', authenticity becomes more easily recognisable because we are now more mobile within a 'fabric of relationships ... [and] ... a person is always located at nodal points.' We are, he claims, all capable of taking part in *some* language games within which novel moves can be made but we only come to temporary resting places and human freedom becomes the freedom to be permanently making other moves. As a result, temporary contractual relationships become a cultural norm and we never arrive at absolute or permanent authenticity. We might each be a player in a language game but most are in very minor leagues, while the major discourses are beyond reach under the control 'of experts of all stripes' (Lyotard, 1979: 15).

Taylor (1992: 35) reinforces this pessimistic view by pointing out that in order to define ourselves we need 'as background, some sense of what is significant in my difference from others,' but when all social indicators are fluid we become less sure of ourselves. 'Horizons of significance' are blurred and we fly blind. 'Significant for me' becomes the only criterion and individuality becomes expressible in trivial and bizarre ways — each deemed equally worthy because they are self-selected. But the result is an individualism which is politically worthless.

Some political implications

Both Dworkin and Taylor draw attention to changes in democratic politics and they reflect two things. One is a growing pre-occupation with the procedural functions of government as part of a process of 'rolling back the State.' At most, the function of government is to provide regulating frameworks rather than a vision of the future and it is particularly manifest in Britain today that Parliament is an institution for pushing through legislation without much debate. The second change is an increasing reliance on judicial review as a means of testing executive decisions. The courts rather than opposition parties are the mechanisms for challenging legislation.

In the USA, judicial review is written into the Constitution, therefore at one level the courts are taking the constitution as a datum. The question is simply whether a piece of legislation is consistent with the constitution. The position in practice is not so clear-cut because there are what Dworkin (1986: 35) refers to as 'interpretive' and non-interpretive theories of judicial review,' and the liberal tradition must favour the former because it is more open-ended. As Dworkin rightly says, 'no-one proposes judicial review as if on a clean slate.' Law itself has a history and a tradition and successive reviews build on previous interpretations in the light of current circumstances. Constitutions, like the Bible, have a fixed text but a changing significance or meaning.

Interpretation by the courts is therefore a dual process of interpreting the constitution and also the new legislation in the light of the first interpretation. However, the courts may not influence or make substantive political decisions which are the prerogative of democratically elected politicians. This is a delicate line to tread and Dworkin (1986: 58) quotes the following principles to be observed:

i)   judicial review should be a matter of attending to the *process* of legislation rather than the outcomes considered in isolation from that process (my italics);

ii)   it should test that process against the standard of democracy.

This is pure deontological liberalism. It is concerned with the regulation of governmental powers and it emphasises process. In such a system, it is the manner in which executive decisions are arrived at which legitimates them rather than any moral content which might be involved and it is the *procedures* which are normative for the system. The basis of this system might be called a 'procedural concept of justice', or as Agnes Heller (1987: 231) describes it, 'dynamic justice' which adapts to changing circumstances. No-one can forecast what form future judicial decisions will take beyond expecting them to conform to the tradition within which the system was developed and it is another example of liberalism in tension. The judicial review system is open-sided and creative yet constrained procedurally.

There is still a further question, however, about the nature of democracy which is one of Dworkin's procedural standards. The question is raised by John Ely who is quoted by Dworkin. He questions the normative principle itself by questioning whether there is one correct conception of 'democracy' on which to judge both judicial and political decisions and the answer is that there cannot be. There appear to be two reasons for this — one empirical and the other theoretical.

Empirically there is no agreed consensus on the precise nature of 'democracy', nor could there be without erecting the concept on absolute value or 'good' and this is theoretically unacceptable. Successive generations must be allowed to make their own interpretation. But the consequence of this must be that the courts, in making decisions on what counts as democracy do what they should not do. The courts engage in substantive politics by defining for the present, what democracy is.

These points reinforce the general contention that deontological liberalism hovers between not wishing to admit the possibility of absolute values while retaining such values in order to provide a substantive frame of reference. This difficulty can, it seems, be resolved only by recognising that we are brought back to political decisions at every turn. This is why the liberal tradition throughout the twists and turns of its history has one central theme which helps to define the tradition. That theme is the containment and control of power with a strong preference for doing so by diffusing or distributing power.

If we ask why there is this preference, we introduce yet more foundational values, such concepts as liberty, freedom, equality, rights, justice and law. If we then ask, 'Why these particular values?' the answer surely must be that behind these there is a commitment to preserving something called 'individuality' and I suggest that this commitment is the basic criterion for placing particular theories and practices within the liberal tradition.

As I have tried to show in this briefest of sketches, there are various ways of looking at the nature of 'individuality' which, like 'democracy', is open to interpretation and alternative definition. It can also be given different weightings in relation to the equally ambiguous concept of 'society.'

'The tradition' that has been the subject of this essay can never, on its own terms, provide absolute answers to any of our questions or to its own, and that is why it is a tradition and not a finite system. It cannot be the latter without producing a totally coherent philosophical case which immediately destroys its own premise that there should not be such a case because it would be inconsistent with individuality and liberty.

But as we have observed, there is one fundamental principle to be preserved and that is the moral commitment to 'individuality,' and this is a practical as well as a theoretical issue. This gives us reason to conclude that moral ideas and politics intertwine with each other and with philosophy which clarifies and defines, but of itself cannot provide foundations, partly because it is unable to do so but also because the liberal tradition cannot allow it to do so.

The change of emphasis from individuality to individualism reduces the possibility of shared values or at least it reduces their number. In doing so, this makes the question of values much more a matter of private concern. 'Individualism' defined as a move to absolute autonomy or authenticity reduces the area of the self by squeezing out the social dimension and reducing the 'horizon of significance'. In diminishing the self, as Agnes Heller (1987: 304) expresses it, 'the more we liberate ourselves from all norms, the more we proceed with the unmaking of the self, the more we become unfree [and] ... the person left without norms, without authorities' ceases to have any grounds on which to reason. Like MacIntyre's person, he or she is reduced to 'I want' and is driven like the child by external stimuli and at random.

We might ask whether the liberal tradition has reached its outer limits with individualism and a radically instead of a socially located self. I suggest that it has and is in danger of destroying itself. For today's individualist this might not matter except for the fact that it is only within society and its norms can there be any notion of rights or of institutions to uphold them. Minimal government on deonotological lines can do that job but a minimal society with minimal values is a different matter. It cannot under any circumstances have a meaningful vision.

Liberalism in adult education

There is a very extensive literature on the concept of liberal adult education and in this concluding section it is intended to do no more than illustrate points of contact with the political liberal tradition.

Within the tradition of analytical philosophy of education (A.P.E.) the impression is often given that liberal education is the only form of true education. R.W.K. Paterson (1979: 38) was thus able to say that 'liberal adult education is not a species of education, it *is* education.' (my italics). But such claims can only be made within the liberal tradition which requires a form of education consonant with the idea of a liberal person as 'autonomous' or 'free' in some sense of that word. Claims of universality for liberal education can only be made if it is assumed that liberal values are themselves universal. Empirically, this clearly is not the case, neither is there a single definition of 'liberalism' and that is our reason for referring to a 'tradition'.

The Great Tradition, as debated and expounded by H.C. Wiltshire (1956 and 1976: 31), was context-bound, especially in the way in which 'education for citizenship' and the idea of 'individuals as social beings' were given prominence. When we put together with A.P.E. concepts of liberal education such as the development of persons, the development of autonomy and of understanding, based on the forms of knowledge, we have what I call a 'classical concept' of liberal adult education because of its affinities with the ideals of Classical Greece. Many of these ideals entered the adult education canon via such writers as

Cardinal Newman, whose ideas have elsewhere been shown to have affinities with the writings of H.C.Wiltshire (see A.H. Thornton, 1976).

The central point about the classical tradition for our present purpose is the idea of autonomy and freedom as being generated within, and as a result of, committed membership of a society with shared values. It is these which are a normative pre-condition for the liberal ideas of freedom and autonomy. Individuality is explicable only in terms of community.

Connections between classical liberal adult education and Mill are also apparent. Mill's individuals were held to have responsibility for the interests of others and the furtherance of such interests provided the only valid reason for interfering with the sovereignty of individuals.

In these various ways classical liberal education was a counterpoint to political and social concepts.

A marked contrast may be seen in 'modern' or deonotological liberalism which stresses 'rights' rather than social responsibility and explicitly rejects the idea of a 'public good'. This is liberalism which is in harmony with views of adult education which have been described as 'libertarian', and having an affinity with existentialism. To some extent, although based on other grounds, Knowles' theories of andragogy point in the same direction by concentrating upon 'self-direction'.

Deonotological principles are implicit in adult education slogans such as 'student choice, personal growth and 'process before content,' all of which represent attempts to be value-free. Choices about learning are legitimised by personal preferences rather than by conformity with normative values. The logic is MacIntyre's 'I want' rather than 'I ought' although this argument does not itself preclude the possibility that choices can and might be made from an existing menu of socially-expressed values. The only requirement is that they need not be.

In practice, a menu of educational 'offerings' is common in adult education and choice is confined to 'which one' of the options on offer. It is the logic of the market place and education is a commodity to be purchased, rather than a public good.

This is all consistent with the deonotological form of liberalism which implicitly postulates a plurality of values, none of which are binding, beyond the value of 'self' and the rights maintaining procedures, which enshrine a procedural concept of justice.

There is a remarkable congruity between theory and practice, indicating and illustrating the manner in which each informs and reinforces the other in a dynamic way, and has the idea of 'change' incorporated within it. To that extent, the deonotological view is well within the liberal tradition which has become very open-ended and liberating in one respect, but there is a false freedom to the extent that choice, from an individual point of view is criterionless, except in the limited sense that a given choice creates, or is seen to have the potential for creating, personal satisfaction.

We might ask whether this position represents a terminus for the liberal tradition, which having eschewed even the desirability as well as the possibility of a public good, can have no vision of its future. Logically, it appears to have two main options. The first is to move towards a plurality of values which is totally disintegrating. The second, which may well follow the first, is to retreat to a more normative position which constrains the expression of individuality and might well become authoritarian.

The liberal tradition is locked into its tensions because they are inherent in its original presuppositions, namely, that there must be government, but government must be contained within limits. Liberal adult education faces a similar dilemma. It seeks to be open and value-free, but values are necessary in order that choices might be meaningful and deemed rational. Some degree of social cohesion and purpose is a necessary condition for its existence and the resolution of this tension is a very political issue.

References

Den Vyl, D. and Rasmussen, D. (1982). Nozick on the Randian Argument. In *Reading Nozick* (ed. P. Jeffrey). Oxford: Basil Blackwell.

Dworkin, R. (1986). *A Matter of Principle*. Oxford: Oxford University Press.

Farrar, C. (1988). *The Origins of Democratic Thinking*. Cambridge: Cambridge University Press.

Heller, A. (1987). *Beyond Justice*. Oxford: Basil Blackwell.

Kitto, H.D.F. (1964). *The Greeks*. Penguin Books.

Lawson, K.H. (1985). Deontological liberalism: the political philosophy of liberal adult education. *Journal of Lifelong Education*, Vol. 4, No. 3.

Locke, J. (1698; 1956). Second Treatise On Civil Government. In *Social Contract* (ed. Sir Ernest Barker). Oxford: Oxford University Press.

Lyotard, J-F. (1979). *The Postmodern Condition* (trans. G. Bennington and B. Massomi). Manchester: Manchester University Press.

MacIntyre, A. (1988). *Whose Justice, Which Rationality?* London: Duckworth.

MacPherson, C.B. (1962). *The Political Theory of Possessive Individualism: Hobbes to Locke.* Oxford: Oxford University Press.

Mill, J.S. (1859; 1962). Utilitarianism. In *Utilitarianism* (ed. M. Warnock). London: Fontana Press.

Nagel, T. (1982). Libertarianism Without Foundations. In *Reading Nozick* (ed. P. Jeffrey). Oxford: Basil Blackwell.

Nozick, R. (1974). *Anarchy, State and Utopia.* Oxford: Basil Blackwell.

Nozick, R. (1982). On the Randian Argument. In *Reading Nozick* (ed. P. Jeffrey). Oxford: Basil Blackwell.

Paterson, R.W.K. (1979). *Values, Education and the Adult.* London: Routledge & Kegan Paul.

Rawls, J. (1972). *A Theory of Justice.* Oxford: Oxford University Press.

Sabine, G.H. (1949). *A History of Political Theory.* London: Harrop.

Taylor, C. (1992). *The Ethics of Authenticity.* Harvard: Harvard University Press.

Thornton, A.H. (1976). Some reflections on the great tradition. In *The Spirit and the Form* (ed. A. Rogers). Nottingham: Department of Adult Education, University of Nottingham.

Toulmin, S. (1961). *Reason in Ethics.* Cambridge: Cambrdige University Press.

Wiltshire, H. (1956). The great tradition in university adult education. *Adult Education,* XXIX, 2. Reprinted in *The Spirit and the Form* (ed. A. Rogers, 1976). Department of Adult Education, University of Nottingham.

Wittgenstein, L. (1958). *Philosophical Investigations* (second edition) (trans. G.E.M. Anscombe). Oxford: Basil Blackwell.

Liberal Adult Education and the Postmodern Moment

R. Usher and R. Edwards

Liberal adult education both as a form of provision and as a justificatory discourse for certain educational practices currently finds itself in a state of crisis and under challenge from a variety of contemporary trends and critiques. In the field, there are mixed reactions to this crisis. There are those for whom the potential loss of liberal adult education is welcome since it helps clear the way for a more 'business-like', vocationally-oriented and less marginalised adult education. Others, grounded at the opposite end of the ideological spectrum, see liberal adult education as oppressively elitist and patriarchal and again would not be unhappy to see its demise. For others still, perhaps a minority, and mainly located in the extra-mural departments of the old universities where the so-called liberal tradition has always been seen as an inherently good thing, its loss or even its undermining through certification represents a significant limitation of the opportunities open to adults. For many, there is a certain nostalgic regret for the imminent passing away of something which whatever its weaknesses has had nevertheless an important formative influence, coupled however with a recognition that liberal adult education has perhaps run its course as a dominant form.

In this chapter, it is not our purpose to identify specifically with any of these positions. However, we do want to argue that liberal adult education, although in a state of crisis, is far from dead and hence we believe that it is still important to question its place in the current conjuncture. Drawing on current debates over the extent to which this marks a distinctive set of economic, social and cultural changes in the social formation — what is often termed the postmodern moment — this chapter will attempt to chart some of the significant dimensions of the current crisis in liberal adult education. We will suggest the need for alternative discourses and practices within the context of the postmodern moment which whilst perhaps not entirely replacing any sense of loss nonetheless present adult education with different, more pleasurable, although possibly troubling challenges.

A word of caution is necessary at this point as we need to at least attempt to say what we mean by liberal adult education and since it is not monolithic this is no easy task. In reality, many stories are told of its values and purposes, this itself indicating a certain degree of uncertainty, diversity and contestation of meaning. Usually, however, these stories do tend to have a common theme insofar as they all speak of the value of learning 'for its own sake', the pursuit of knowledge untrammelled by the pressures of certification or work preparation — education as an end in itself which yet helps to bring about personal development, fulfil individual autonomy and need, build confidence and redress disadvantage. These stories present meanings which provide a normative base for a variety of pedagogic practices and curricular aims.

In the UK, liberal adult education is historically associated with non-certificated, non-vocational learning opportunities taken in leisure time. Such opportunities have largely been structured through local authority adult education, the WEA and the extra-mural departments of the old universities. In this connection it is worth noting that the meaning of 'liberal' in local authority adult education has always differed from that prevalent in the other two modes of provision. In the latter, 'liberal' did not simply mean an uncertificated, leisure-time provision but also one that was supposed to involve rigorous, discipline-based study at university-level or equivalent. At the same time, even this meaning of 'liberal' has not been uncontested. The privileging in adult education of 'experience' has involved a rejection or at the least a questioning of discipline-based learning in favour of experience and experiential learning as the basis of the educational event.

Despite these contested meanings, the current crisis is generally seen as largely stemming from the policies since 1979 of successive Conservative governments, policies which have sought to harness education in all sectors more directly to economic policy and the perceived need to increase the competitiveness of the British economy.

Governments' preferred means of bringing this about has been to stress the priority of labour market needs and to make all sectors of education both 'market-led' and 'market-like' (see Ball, 1990; Kenway et al., 1993). For the adult education sector, this policy has had paradoxical results. On the one hand, it has led to an increasing interest in and support for adult learners and the provision of learning opportunities — an expansion of opportunity. On the other hand, that interest is largely focused on providing certificated opportunities relevant to the labour market. Funding and consequently provision has therefore moved towards the vocational and the certificated with the non-vocational and the non-certificated being required to recover a much larger proportion of their direct and indirect costs through student fee-income. The leisurely pursuit of learning for its own sake, in principle available to all at subsidised cost, has virtually disappeared. Instrumental learning for work and qualifications coupled with the increasing prevalence of competency-based curricula — in other words, adult education as training and competence — have now become the primary agenda for an increasing diversity of providers of adult learning opportunities. Education as an end in itself has been marginalised as greater emphasis is placed on the fulfilment of certain instrumental goals.

For many in the field therefore, it is the lack of support from government for liberal adult education which is seen as the prime cause of the current crisis. However, in our view, to see things this way is misleading since firstly, it fails to relate educational developments to wider social trends and secondly, it displaces and to some extent conceals concerns rooted in the very nature of the practice of liberal adult education — concerns about who it serves and for what purpose. These concerns about access, pedagogy and curriculum have been raised for some time now by a variety of critics of the traditional, discipline-based form of liberal adult education.

As we have noted earlier, those who emphasise the place of 'experience' in adult education have conceptualised it as the foundation and most important resource for learning, the centre of knowledge-production and processes of knowledge acquisition. To this extent, they are able to offer a powerful critique of discipline-based liberal adult education by stressing the importance of the experience of the learner (learning from experience) and the *process* of learning (experiential learning). However, a number of problematic elements are discernible in this approach. First, the replacement of canonical knowledge as the foundation of learning with experience does not replace foundationalism and the experiential approach therefore remains trapped in a discourse of foundations. Second, given that experience is portrayed as the source or origin of knowledge the emphasis is therefore placed on the knowledge or learning that emerges from it rather than on experience itself. Consequently, experience is unproblematised, taken as a 'given', with a failure to recognise that experience is produced and its meaning always contested and contestable. Third, even when this is taken into account, the learning or knowledge which emerges from experience and the process of experiential learning is fitted into a pre-given universal framework which defines what outcomes are desirable and which processes are congruent with their attainment (for example, the emphasis on the universal efficacy of facilitation).

Another critical strand is that associated with socialist/Marxist, feminist and anti-racist members of the adult education community (Thompson, 1983; Parsons, 1990; Hart, 1992; McGivney, 1992). Here the critique of liberal adult education was that its predominantly white middle-class orientation offered a curriculum which largely serviced and reinforced women's domestic and subordinate roles in the workplace. Such critics questioned the adequacy of the justificatory story which liberal adult education purveyed.

It is not so much that the notion of 'social purpose' has been lacking in liberal adult education. On the contrary, such a commitment has always been present, albeit as a minority tendency. However, as Benn and Fieldhouse (1994) point out, the commitment to emancipation and social equality has always been diluted by the even stronger commitment to university standards and 'objective' knowledge, particularly amongst extra-mural practitioners. The dominant emphasis in liberal adult education on personal development and learning for its own sake has inscribed notions of the disinterested pursuit of knowledge, with both access and curricula based on the opportunity to participate in and assimilate a pre-existing canon of knowledge. What emphasis there was on social purpose was inscribed in *universal* notions of social equality and emancipation in the provision of 'really useful knowledge' for the working class. However, even here, the radical discourse in effect gave rise to practices privileging the interests of particular sections of the social formation, predominantly the white, male, unionised working class.

More recently, the notion of 'social purpose' has been increasingly re-defined and distanced from the 'liberal' element through an ideology critique that foregrounds the structural inequalities inherent in the patriarchal individualism of the liberal tradition. However, there still remains a coalescing of interests in the emphasis on uncertificated, non-vocational learning and a common self-understanding of the task of adult education as a 'mission' dedicated to the cause of social 'progress' through learning.

Even though learning and individual development has been redefined by the different radical strands within a context of experiential learning, social development and social equality, the 'unreconstructed' liberals, the experientialists and other radicals still all speak the same language, still tell mutually intelligible stories and still work within the same broad parameters. We would argue that they all are still rooted in the modernist project of education, all still see themselves as bearers of universal 'messages', all define what they do through the 'grand narratives' or overarching legitimating stories of modernity.

Modernity and postmodernity

At this point it is appropriate to say something about current notions of modernity and postmodernity. At its simplest level, modernity can be understood as a historical period with its origins in the Enlightenment and continuing to the present day. The Enlightenment marked the beginnings of the process of modernisation, of economic and socio-cultural change and disruption marked by 'industrialisation, the growth of science and technology, the modern state, the capitalist world market, urbanisation and other infrastructural elements' (Featherstone, 1991: 60). Alongside these developments went such cultural changes as secularisation and an emphasis on personal identity and autonomy.

Postmodernity, on the other hand, is associated with such contemporary trends as the growth of service-sector employment, 'post-industrial' social formations and post-Fordist modes of production, and globalisation. Here developments in information technology, the media and transportation are particularly significant as they have resulted in increased space-time compression and global integration (Edwards, 1994). Whilst such trends have a complex history and geography of their own, the development of globalisation is an aspect of a contemporary situation marked by the 'compression of the world and the intensification of consciousness of the world as a whole' (Robertson, 1992: 8). Robertson terms the contemporary situation an 'uncertainty phase' where global consciousness has heightened, with international systems more fluid, the prospects for humanity more fraught in the light of environmental and other risks.

There is general agreement about the overall process of globalisation and the significance of the speed of communication to that process — the phenomenon of 'everything that happens in the world we know about in five minutes'. In many ways it is the development of communications in its widest sense which has underpinned globalisation, as information about and from around the globe is gained directly through travel and indirectly yet increasingly instantly through electronic media — through satellite television and the rapidly developing information 'superhighway'. The world therefore enters our homes in the media we engage with and the products we consume. It is the re-valuing of consumption and the consumer which marks the shift in emphasis between modernity and postmodernity.

One consequence of the trend to consumption has been the slow demise of modernist centres of production — the factory, the assembly-line, large-scale manufacturing — and their replacement by centres of consumption — niche marketing, small-scale specialised enterprises, financial services, shopping malls and superstores, entertainment centres and theme parks. Out of this breakdown and transformation of modernist, production-oriented identity, it is argued, emerges a postmodern consumption-oriented identity, although this is an argument that remains contested (see Field, 1994).

With these trends towards global integration and in response to them, and with the emergence of postmodern identities, the white, Western male cultural assumptions found within modernist normative discourses of humanity and society have been problematised by among other things considerations of gender, sexual, ethnic and racial differences. New ideas and fresh conceptualisations, new discourses such as feminist, post-colonial and 'green' discourses have been found necessary to help explain the contemporary condition and it is these new discourses and their associated practices which have emerged in the postmodern moment.

The discourses and practices of modernity are characterised by an emphasis on progress and a faith in rationality and science as the means of its realisation. This faith with its promise of inevitable progress in human betterment is a feature of modernity which perhaps is most intensely questioned in the postmodern moment. Lyotard (1984) refers to the idea of human betterment and social progress through scientific knowledge as one of the 'grand narratives', the higher-order forms of legitimation which in postmodernity are increasingly greeted with 'incredulity'. This incredulity, scepticism or general loss of faith arises, as Johnson (1994: 7) argues, because of the obvious and glaring discrepancy between modernity's 'humanistic concepts of freedom, justice, rationality, and equality that the West has promoted and the actual forms of oppression and domination (slavery, anti-semitism, colonialism, sexual inequality, racism and so on) in which the West has engaged'.

Postmodernity then is characterised by a questioning of the scientific attitude, a denial of the universal efficacy of technical/instrumental reason and scientific method and of the stance of objectivity and value-neutrality in the making of knowledge claims. Here it is not a matter of rejecting these but rather of seeing them as socially-formed, historically-located cultural constructs and thus partial and specific to particular discourses and purposes. They need also to be seen as totalising power plays since they conceal themselves in the cloak of universality, value-neutrality and benevolent progress. This feature is not confined to liberal humanist discourse. Even Marxist discourse with its claims for a scientific basis of analysis constructs the working class as the bearer of the universal interests of humanity against the partial interests of capital and is thus implicated in the limits of modernity. In modernity, it is always the 'other' who is 'partial'!

In postmodernity, the recognition of the significance of language, discourse and socio-cultural locatedness in any knowledge claim leads to a questioning of universal and transcendental foundations and canonical forms of knowledge. This has had paradoxical consequences. On the one hand, it has resulted in an erosion of the 'liberal' curriculum and an emphasis on the provision of learning opportunities which optimise the efficiency of the economic and social system. On the other, it has resulted in a valuing of different sources and forms of knowledge, a reconfiguration of the meaning of 'liberal'. The emphasis on experiential learning is an example of this although, as we have noted, its apparent break with modernity is attenuated by its modernist self-understandings. What all these consequences have in common is that they both reflect and give rise to greater uncertainty and conflict over the power and purpose of education.

To a large extent these trends can be seen as a 'decentring' of knowledge, the effect of which is to contribute to the undermining of modernist certainty with consequent uncertainty pervading thought, action and identity. As we have noted earlier, postmodernity is a condition where people have to make their way without fixed referents and traditional anchoring points in a world characterised by rapid change and bewildering instability, where knowledge is not only constantly changing but is becoming more rapidly and overwhelmingly available and where meaning 'floats'. A modernist perspective views all this with an existential anxiety and with profound concern, a postmodern perspective as a matter of celebration of diversity and difference, of troubled pleasure.

Postmodernity has also been termed a condition of 'hyper-commodification' (Crook et al., 1992), the condition where the commodity has become culturally dominant (Kenway et al. 1993) and where the dominant commodity form is the image. Hence the increased dominance of consumption, particularly of images, and the consumer. The communication/media revolution which we discussed earlier means that people are engulfed by images to the extent where the distinction between reality and image breaks down in a condition of 'hyperreality' (Baudrillard, 1988). The hyperreal is a world of constantly proliferating images or 'simulacra' (copies detached from their originals but meaningful despite this detachment) which become a desirable reality to be consumed and where experience is random and contingent rather than coherent and determinate. In this process, new forms of experience proliferate, experiences that are not rooted in a stable and unified self. Hence there is continual shaping and re-shaping of subjectivity and identity. In postmodernity therefore sensibilities are attuned to the pleasure of constant and new experiencing where experiencing becomes its own end rather than a means to an end, part of a constant making and re-making of a 'life-style'— a process of 'cruising' (Turner, 1993) that is best summed up in Baudrillard's comment that 'the further you travel the more clearly you realise that the journey is all that matters' (Baudrillard, 1990: 168). In the postmodern moment, the cultivation of desire replaces modernity's cultivation of reason (Usher and Edwards, 1994).

In postmodernity therefore the decentring of knowledge is accompanied by a decentring of the self. Modernity is characterised by a search for an underlying and unifying truth and certainty which will make the world and the self coherent, meaningful and masterable. In modernity, although the self constantly experiences a sense of discontinuity and fragmentation, this however is regarded as an 'unnatural' condition to be remedied by such practices as counselling and adult education which enable the uncovering of a pre-existing coherent and authentic self. Postmodernity, on the contrary, is marked by 'a view of the human world as irreducibly and irrevocably pluralistic, split into a multitude of sovereign units and sites of authority' (Bauman, 1992: 35). The modernist search for a true and authentic self and the fulfilment of a pre-given individual autonomy gives way to a 'playfulness' where identity is formed (and re-formed) by a constantly unfolding desire realised, although never fully and finally, through life-style 'cruising' in its multiplicity of forms. The unified, coherent and sovereign self of modernity, the firm ground for the fixing of identity, becomes a multiple, discontinuous, self traversed by multiple meanings and whose identity is continually in a process of re-formation. In postmodernity, one does not experience in order to enumerate the knowledge gained or to become a 'better' person or to better become oneself. Experience leads to further experience, experiencing is itself the end, not the means to an end. It is the very openness of experience which is desirable.

The challenge to education

As both a generator of knowledge through research and its transmission through dedicated institutions educational discourses and practices have had a powerful role in the development, maintenance and legitimation of modernity. Education is the site where ideals of critical reason, individual autonomy and benevolent progress are disseminated and internalised — the site where the project of modernity can be realised. As we have noted, this project as embodied in the grand narratives emphasises mastering the world in the cause of human betterment by means of 'objective' knowledge generated by rational scientific approaches. In modernity, mastery *is* progress where individual enlightenment and social and material development, individual emancipation and democracy are seen as mutually interactive and reinforcing.

Although there have always been profound disagreements over curricular means and the particular forms education should take, educational practices are legitimated and shaped by this grand narrative of progress and emancipation through the mastery of knowledge and of knowledge that masters. Modernity's project of mastery can therefore be seen as a kind of benevolent and generally implicit social engineering where progress has a certain meaning and functions both as a pre-given end which education strives for and the norm by which it is judged.

The main task for education in fulfilling the project of modernity is the forming and shaping of the kind of subjectivity and sense of identity that we have described earlier. This is a task which also preoccupies liberal adult education in all its variants. In an important sense, its goals, definition of needs, curriculum, pedagogy and organisational forms are implicitly structured by the social engineering of the project of modernity. It is one of the ways in which the message of modernity is delivered. The grand narratives are therefore inscribed in the very practices of liberal adult education. Thus the contemporary crisis of liberal adult education can be seen as a microcosm of the more general crisis of modernity which we are part of at this the postmodern moment.

Consequently, it's clear that education does not fit easily into postmodernity. There are a number of reasons for this. Firstly, given that in the postmodern moment there is 'a much more ambivalent and less fixed positioning of subjectivity' (Lash 1991: 198), the 'decentred' self challenges both the assumption of the bounded 'natural' self with inherent potential and the goal of personal autonomy which is at the heart of education. If the self can no longer be conceived as a container (see Sampson, 1993) filled with innate qualities but is rather socially, discursively, and intersubjectively constructed then the assumptions of possessive individualism which underlie all forms of 'liberal' education are undermined. This is why in the postmodern moment there is a celebration rather than suppression of the 'other' or the radically different, and why the implicit acceptance of the white, male middle-class norm is rendered problematic. Furthermore, autonomy is not something to be attained 'self-ishly' but relationally through a recognition of difference where differences are not the basis for the ascription of deficits.

Secondly, in questioning the status and indeed the very existence of foundational knowledge there is also a challenge to scientific rationality, to existing concepts, structures and hierarchies of knowledge and to the part education plays in maintaining and reproducing these. If there are no sure foundations and no Archimedean points from which knowledge is generated and assimilated but instead a plurality of partial knowledges, then the very foundations of discipline-based education are themselves undermined. Without foundations and an absolute faith in scientificity, the certainty and determinacy for which modernity strives is no longer so certain and with this a curriculum based on the dissemination of 'true' and certain knowledge becomes highly problematic.

Thirdly, and this is a point we shall return to again later, the undermining of the modernist project of education undermines the grand narrative of progress and hence the meaning of progress which that narrative embodies and disseminates. As we have noted, progress means change which fulfils certain pre-defined ends. In the project of modernity progress is judged by such things as a greater mastery of the physical and social world, the growth of scientific knowledge, the spread of a particular kind of rationality and the development of the rational, enlightened and autonomous person. Anything which fulfils these ends is deemed 'good' i.e. 'progressive', everything which doesn't 'bad' i.e. retrogressive. The modernist project tells us *in advance* what is universally good for us, what we should be aiming for and how we can best attain it. In other words, the notion of 'progress' is both teleological and totalising. Anything which doesn't fall under these definitions becomes a feared and rejected 'other' to be ignored, marginalised, derided or suppressed. It is for this reason then that in the postmodern moment 'progress' is subjected to a serious critique which highlights the possibility of change without teleology, an alternative notion of change outside the totalising modernist project where change, at either the personal or social level, can take a multiplicity of forms and fulfil a variety of ends or even simply be its own end.

Liberal adult education and modernity

Postmodernity therefore, by rendering liberal adult education problematic, engenders the state of crisis which adult educators increasingly feel and which they express in terms of something lacking in the present, a loss of something valuable. This normally takes two forms. First, the loss of opportunities for people to learn for its own sake without instrumental, vocational goals and without the need for accreditation and second, the loss of a commitment to social purpose and transformation in the work of adult educators. Often these two strands interweave. What these expressions of loss signify is the *investment* in liberal adult education which its practitioners have - in other words, that the commitment to liberal adult education is not simply a matter of rational calculation, conservatism or pragmatism. This perhaps explains why adult educators in the liberal tradition tend to regard their work as a 'mission' and why they feel a sense of loss in the present and a nostalgia for an imagined past where personal development and social purpose were the clear and uncontentious aspirations and goals of adult education. Thus rather than looking forward to filling the lack by harnessing the potential and possibilities of the present and the rapidly emerging future they tend to focus backward to a lack created by a feared and omnipotent 'Other'.

However, although the existence of an investment is significant the consequent feelings of loss and nostalgia are invested in an *imagined* past and this tends to obscure the genealogy of adult education and its position within specific socio-economic and cultural contexts. For example, it could be argued that the liberal tradition of education 'for its own sake' has never been a significant form, nor indeed that the notion of 'education for its own sake' has ever been a significant feature of this tradition. The roots of the notion of education, or perhaps more accurately 'learning', for its own sake rather lie in the practices of the aristocracy and the notion of the cultivated 'gentleman' of leisure (and here it is important to note the sexist and classist connotations of this term) whose social position, although not a function of educational background, involved the cultivation of certain broad 'educative' learning experiences.

Raymond Williams (1962) has pointed out that the particular way in which education developed in the nineteenth century can be understood in terms of the conflict between 'old humanists' and 'public educators'. The former were members (white men) of the leisured class for whom aristocratic cultural values were paramount and for whom the possibility of being educated could be open only to an elite. They were therefore opposed to mass schooling. The latter in contrast were committed to individual and social development through education available to all — hence they were ardent proponents of mass schooling. It was largely through their influence that the notion of a modern meritocratic society and of individual mobility through education was inscribed in the discourses of the emerging education profession.

However, in an ironic twist which helps us to understand some of our contemporary paradoxes, 'public educators' drew on the arguments of the 'old humanists' in their conflict with the 'industrial trainers' who saw education solely as direct preparation for work. Both the 'public educators' and the 'industrial trainers' wanted universal education but the former were profoundly opposed to the latter's narrow vocationalism. There was therefore a coming together of the 'old humanists' and the 'public educators' with the latter adopting the former's notions of liberal education, the cultivation of the intellect and learning 'for its own sake' grounded in academic scholarship. This coming together helped to define a specific terrain for the development of a particular form of universal education which has dogged Britain with its constant re-inscribing of value in institutions and curricula which exclude the achievements of the less powerful majority from due recognition.

As the main institutionalised form of universal education, mass schooling could never be entirely insulated from the instrumental demands of state and economy and hence from vocationalism and certification. Adult education on the other hand as a marginal form was able to take an ostensibly more 'liberal' path and adopt some elements of the 'learning for its own sake' tradition of the 'old humanists'. Thus the paradox mentioned above was manifested in the practices of the early extension movement of the old universities which literally attempted to take academic scholarship and an elite non-vocational Oxbridge culture to some sections of the wider community. What this clearly shows is that the non-instrumental nature of the liberal tradition in adult education actually has its basis in the aristocratic values, class and patriarchal position of the 'old humanists' even though these values were overlaid with a more democratic ethos. This complex genealogy probably illustrates why adult education has always been a mixture of the democratic and the elitist, the conservative and the radical, the liberating and the oppressive. Since the 'old humanists' were not fully part of the modernist project, but still retained elements of a pre-modern tradition, it also shows why a simplistic picture of liberal adult education as fully modernist is misleading.

The implication of this therefore is that the relationship of liberal adult education to modernity and by extension postmodernity is a complex one. This complexity is a consequence of a general feature that tends to be concealed when modernity is conceived simply as a bounded historical period. Insofar as it could be argued that modernity does not simply comprise a discrete historical period, periodisation does not properly express what is entailed by it. We would agree with Foucault (1986) that it is better not to think in terms of periods or epochs and of changes in these but rather to see pre-modernity, modernity and postmodernity as oppositional attitudes and discourses which can and always are present in any historical period. Postmodernity then does not mark the end or the disappearance of modernity. The modern and indeed the pre-modern are incorporated within the postmodern moment albeit in a consciously reflexive and ironic way.

This provides a useful way of looking at the past, present and future position of liberal adult education. Liberal adult education is clearly rooted in modernity but as we have already hinted it also has certain pre-modern elements. It is within these elements that its non-instrumental, 'learning for its own sake' features are rooted, features which as we shall see recur in postmodernity albeit in a reconfigured form. At the same time, it is possible to argue that liberal adult education *is* instrumental — not in a narrow sense but instrumental nonetheless in the wider sense of being directed towards the fulfilment of the project of modernity — education in the service of modernity, education as a vehicle for the realisation of the grand narratives. Two features of this are discernible. First, education has sought to produce a certain kind of world, a world shaped in the cause of human betterment. Second, it has been education which has sought to create and shape a certain kind of subjectivity, a person with certain kinds of qualities and attitudes rather than certain kinds of work or vocationally oriented skills. It is because of these features that the instrumentality of education is not immediately obvious.

In postmodernity, we are witnessing changes which are bound to lead to a reconfiguration of adult education. The currently popular replacement term 'adult learning' is undoubtedly a symptom of this. It is the liberal tradition which is most effected by this reconfiguration. With the loss of faith in the grand narratives of modernity and the emphasis on the cultivation of desire over the cultivation of reason there comes a questioning of educational forms whose dominant rationale is to service the modernist project. Alternative forms, more in tune with the postmodern moment, are beginning to emerge giving significance to notions of 'edu-tainment' and 'info-cation' and the role of learners as consumers. Yet it would be simplistic to see these as the advance revolutionary guard of a radically different 'postmodern' adult education. Elements of the modern and the pre-modern will still be present albeit in reconfigured forms. This needs to be borne in mind in any evaluation of the significance of adult learning within a context of new (postmodern) stories and practices.

Adult education in the postmodern moment

At this point, it would be appropriate to say something, albeit of a very tentative nature, about the possible characteristics of adult education (or adult learning?) in the postmodern moment. We have characterised one aspect of this moment as an 'incredulity' towards grand narratives. These although far from dead in their effects, given for example the continuing interest and participation in traditional liberal forms of adult learning, have nonetheless lost much of their motivating and justificatory power. The end of education, therefore, as a vehicle for realising the modernist project is one of the main characteristics of education in the postmodern. Coming to an end as a project implies that education can no longer be understood or understand itself as standing above history and particular socio-cultural contexts. It can no longer be solely dedicated, in any of its various forms, to the achievement of progress as pre-defined by the grand narratives. In the case of adult education, it cannot through its liberal discourse continue any longer as a *concealed* instrumentalism.

A number of consequences follow from this, some of which are already with us. In general terms, educational forms are likely to be more diverse in terms of goals and processes, organisational structures, curricula, pedagogy and participants. Education would take its cue from, although not be determined by, the diverse cultural contexts in which it was located rather than be determined by a set of universal norms. Instead of seeking to reduce everything to the 'same' (e.g. to non-certificated provision, to experiential learning, to education for liberation) it would instead express 'difference' in its diversity and provide space for a diversity of 'voices'.

Foundational knowledge, given its self-understanding that it discovers the 'truth' of an independently existing world, inscribes education in a discourse of predictability and control (the 'mastery' we referred to earlier). The postmodern scepticism of this inscription implies that education is not part of a predictable 'reality' and therefore is neither controlled nor controlling. Given unpredictability, it makes no sense to speak of education as functioning either to reproduce the social order or as a means of implicit social engineering whether this be for domestication or liberation. Thus the polar distinction 'domestication-liberation' would no longer have the same structuring power. Educational sites whilst still sites of power and therefore still contested would be neither determined nor determining. Education therefore escapes the epistemological, political and physical boundaries imposed on it by the project of modernity. The boundaries which differentiated educational institutions from the wider social formation and from each other break down as the disciplinary forms through which knowledge and truth were held to be produced come increasingly into question.

The undermining of foundations makes questionable an educational provision based on any kind of foundation — either one which produces and/or disseminates canonical knowledge, or one which makes experience and facilitation canonical, or even one which canonises such universal terms as 'oppression' and 'liberation. At the same time, education need not simply assume a *single* form, for example, certificated provision or competence-based training, although these would be part of a diversity and plurality of educational offerings. This implies that any attempt to place education into a straitjacket of uniform provision, standardised curricula, technicised teaching and bearer of universal 'messages' of rationality would be difficult to impose. Education in the postmodern is likely to be characterised by different levels and kinds of provision.

Furthermore, modernist education in all its forms has tended to be elitist with a rhetoric of participation but a reality of exclusion. Education in the postmodern, based as it is on cultural contexts, on localised and particularised knowledges, on the cultivation of desire, on the valuing of a multiplicity of experience as an integral part of defining a 'lifestyle', cannot help but construct itself in a form which would better enable greater participation in a diversity of ways by a diversity of learners.

Education in the postmodern moment is characterised therefore by a general decentring of educational authority, control and provision. This is part of a more encompassing trend that loosens and blurs boundaries and demarcations, the 'de-differentiation' which we referred to earlier. In the field of education it implies the breakdown of clear demarcations between different sectors of education and between education and cognate fields. There are two implications here. One is that formally constituted fields of education would find it hard to continue to claim a monopoly since potentially any activity in any context could claim to involve learning and hence be deemed 'educational'. The other is that education need not be so narrowly construed since it would instead be seen as an aspect of life itself. The 'educated person' need no longer be someone who has been credentialled by completing certain 'rites of passage' in formal education institutions. Everyone, in different degrees and in differing ways, is an educated person. In passing, this would open up significant possibilities for the accreditation of prior learning, although perhaps not in the way it is currently constructed.

These then are some of the possible characteristics of the educational form in the postmodern moment. Some are already with us, others may never fully come to pass — for example, the onset of a National Curriculum would seem to be opposed to the trend towards less centralised curricula. Furthermore, as we hinted at earlier, it would be very problematic to see the postmodern moment as inaugurating a time of liberated education and education for liberation even though it involves a reconfiguration of liberal education. The post-industrial order of the postmodern imposes its own disciplines. As many commentators have pointed out (see for example, Ball, 1990; Kenway et al., 1993) the new vocationalism is very much about the transmission of certain types of attitudes and competencies considered appropriate for the 'market' and the emerging post-Fordist world of work. Yet even here this is a reconfigured instrumentalism, it is not the instrumentalism either implicit or explicit of the modernist project. Competence-based education is not designed as a means of creating a 'better' person or of fulfilling a universal end since it can have no purpose in relation to an intrinsic human 'nature' and, since becoming competent is an endless process of adaptation, there is no definable and determinate end which it can fulfil. It has to be seen therefore as socially constructed, historically located with contested meanings and differential investments.

What we are putting forward then are to some extent largely speculations rather than the universal features of a worked-out future. But they do present interesting possibilities with significant implications for the future, suggesting generally a decentring of the educational form which for the reasons we have suggested might actually lead to a more likely fulfilment of that elusive dream of adult education viz. greater accessibility and participation.

All this has obvious implications for a reconfiguration of adult education. Certainly, it is easy to see why 'adult learning' would become a more apt term. It highlights a number of features. First, it implies that learning is not something which can only be considered to be such when it leads to pre-defined outcomes, whatever these outcomes may be. Second, it foregrounds the significant place of learning as against the institutional form or the discursive tradition. Adult educators are reminded that learning is both boundless and contextual, something which they have tended to forget because of the influence of the liberal tradition and despite the importance accorded to experience. Third, this implies that 'adult education' is not confined to the contexts and institutions which are formally labelled as such. Adult learning does not just happen in classrooms or through formal courses but in a variety of contexts, movements, institutions and learning environments e.g. workplaces. Fourth, it suggests that enablers of adult learning are not simply those who have been ascribed this label. This obviously has implication for the notion of professional expertise and for the training and credentialling of adult educators.

In a wider sense, the onset of adult learning as against adult education marks, as Bagnell (1994) points out, a waning of the attitude that the only worthwhile learning is that which is good for you — 'good' being pre-defined in terms of the goals of the modernist project. Learning becomes a matter of desire rather than duty, an autobiographical aspect of the decentred self. This opens up an important role for the use of different media in satisfying the diverse desires of adult learners and it is not surprising that the postmodern moment is characterised by the turn to such media, not only in various forms of open and distance learning, but also through such developments as CD-roms, the Internet and e-mail.

While the impetus behind these developments has been the pursuit of modernist goals and that is certainly how it is characterised in the discourses of open and distance learning, the possibilities its development has unleashed have been far wider and we would argue more significant. Open and distance learning, for example, provides support for the wider processes in the reorganisation of space-time outlined earlier and the satisfaction of diverse desires of a more diverse range of adult learners.

The relationship between learning and face-to-face interaction has been broken and with that, the necessity for people to attend specific places for learning at specific times is undermined. It is the place of the learner — their learning setting — that is foregrounded rather than that of the provider. As geographical dispersal and the compression of space-time through the use and speed of new forms of communication enhance globalisation, learners and providers becoming increasingly 'available' to each other on a global scale through the various forms of media. Evans and Nation (1992: 181) suggest that 'distance education and open learning have been the key dispersal agents' in the movement towards a post-industrial society.

Similarly, with the greater emphasis on the personal identity of the learner and their lifestyle choices, questions are raised as to the adequacy of modernist discourses to provide us with the categories to 'make sense' of learners. Notions of the rational self and human development transcend the actual identities of learners in the postmodern moment. They and the practices they support attempt to constitute learners in this manner, but their power to do so in the face of countervailing trends is increasingly limited and lacking in relevance. As with learners so with learning. If identity is subject to decentring then the ways in which we engage learners may need re-evaluating. Thus, with the proliferation of information technology and media, it may well be that the future cohort will not be addressed primarily through literacy in terms of the written word but that computer and media literacy will be of far greater significance with a greater emphasis on image and information. In this case computers and the media cannot simply be conceived as 'books without covers' but will need to engage the specific desires of learners cultivated through their use.

The future of the crisis

The crisis of liberal adult education in the present period in many ways expresses precisely the loss of faith in the modernist project at this the postmodern moment. However, rather than seeking to address the issues raised by that loss in an open and creative way there is, as we have seen, a reassertion and continuation of what for many has patently failed. This is not to say that liberal adult education has not made its contribution to individuals, groups and organisations. Most adult educators are themselves an illustration of that success. However, whether it has contributed in the ways in which it has expressed this to itself and to others is perhaps a more open question than is often suggested. In the postmodern moment of uncertainty greater scepticism towards the claims of educators and greater modesty while troubling may be no bad thing.

Part of this is to take ourselves and each other less seriously. This is not a call for frivolity but rather a call to take reflexivity more seriously and to recognise the place of desire in the learning event. The role of liberal adult education in contributing to personal development and progressive social change has always been constructed as a serious business, this no doubt being a concomitant of its deep sense of mission. This is probably why such discomfort is expressed about redefining adult education in relation to leisure, about shifts towards consumerism in education as in other areas of life, and about the recent growth in the market and marketing of education opportunities. What this does is devalue a range of learning and learning activities which are not invested with the missionary project of the liberal adult educator. Even more important, it fails to address its own investment of desire in the pursuit of universal individual enlightenment and social purpose. As Weiler (1991) argues, universal claims need to be located in concrete historical and social contexts. This poses a challenge to educators to make clear and reflect upon, as a vital element in the learning process, their own subject positions — or to put it another way their 'situated biographies' — rather than adopting the stance of the disembodied and disembedded bearer of universal 'messages'.

The sense of lack which we have alluded to earlier is therefore in reality the lack of a reflexivity which would allow the liberal adult educator to take pleasure, albeit a troubled pleasure, in 'rewriting' adult education for the contemporary condition. In the main, the contemporary condition is construed simply as troubles devoid of pleasure. Undoubtedly, this troubled state is part of a breakdown of adult educators' sense of a fixed and settled identity with the consequent expressions of loss that we have noted earlier. But it also makes possible the failure to address the inscription of liberal adult education in practices which perpetuate the very inequalities and oppressions which it has traditionally understood itself to be challenging.

In foregrounding the significance of the postmodern moment, we have to be aware also of the dangers. There are, for example, dangers in the process of decentring. Does not someone, somewhere have to assume responsibility for provision, no matter how diverse and contextualised it may be? Furthermore, if everything becomes 'educational' then education in any institutionalised sense could easily end up with no role whatsoever. All these possible dangers are implicated with questions of power. One of the justifications always given for institutionalised adult education is that it provides a power base, however ineffectual this has shown itself to be. The same too is said about the need for a cadre of 'professional' adult educators and a canonical body of adult education knowledge. It is argued that to remove the professionals and to question the status of the body of knowledge would dilute whatever power adult education has and marginalise it even further.

Without wishing to minimise these dangers, it is not unreasonable however to treat the hand-wringing about the dangers which the loss of liberal adult education would bring with a certain amount of scepticism. The historical record of liberal adult education as an effective power base would seem dismal to say the least. Furthermore, with a few honourable exceptions, it has been no friend of adult education as a field of study. Its understanding of individual and social development has been narrow and exclusive. Its sense of a civilising mission has been 'colonial', patriarchal and readily translatable into a smug and narrow-minded self-satisfaction.

Yet as we have mentioned earlier, as adult educators it is not easy to escape its influence — and that is the case for us in common with many others. Furthermore, as we have seen, it would be premature and simplistic to pronounce its demise. Nor indeed would this be appropriate since the diversity of provision that characterises the postmodern moment leaves space for a reconfigured liberal form. Indeed as Bagnell (1994) points out, there is some convergence between adult education in the postmodern moment and the 'old humanist' form of liberal education but without the latter's class location. On the other hand, while we join in the hope of Westwood (1991) for a reframing of adult education in meeting the challenge of the contemporary conjuncture we feel uncertain of that being achieved within the parameters of modernity inscribed in liberal adult education's discourse and practice.

References

Bagnell, R. (1994). Continuing education in postmodernity: four semantic tensions. *International Journal of Lifelong Education*, 13,4: 265-279.

Ball, S. (1990). *Politics and Policy Making in Education*. London: Routledge.

Baudrillard, J. (1988). *Selected Works* (ed. M. Poster). Cambridge: Polity Press.

Baudrillard, J. (1990). *Cool Memories*. London: Verso.

Bauman, Z. (1992). *Intimations of Postmodernity*. London: Routledge.

Benn, R. and Fieldhouse, R. (1994). Raybouldism, Russell and New Reality. In *Reflecting on Changing Practices, Contexts and Identities* (eds. P. Armstrong, B. Bright, and M. Zukas). Hull: SCUTREA.

Crook, S., Paluski, J., and Waters, M. (1992). *Postmodernisation*. London: Sage.

Edwards, R. (1994). From a distance: globalisation, space-time compression and distance education. *Open Learning*, 9,3.

Evans, T. and Nation, D. (1992). Theorising open and distance education. *Open Learning*, 7,2: 3-13.

Featherstone, M. (1991). *Consumer Culture and Postmodernism*. London: Sage.

Field, J. (1994). Open learning and consumer culture. *Open Learning*, 9,2: 3-11.

Foucault, M. (1986). What is Enlightenment? In *The Foucault Reader* (ed. P. Rabinow). Harmondsworth: Peregrine Books.

Hart, M. (1992). *Working and Educating for Life: Feminist and International Perspectives on Adult Education*. London: Routledge.

Johnson, B. (1994). Introduction. In *Freedom and Interpretation* (ed B. Johnson). New York: Basic Books.

Kenway, J., Bigum, C., and Fitzclarence, L. (1993). Marketing education in the postmodern age. *Journal of Education Policy*, 8,2: 105-122.

Lash, S. (1991). *Sociology of Postmodernism*. London: Routledge.

Lyotard, J.F. (1984). *The Postmodern Condition: A Report on Knowledge*. Manchester: Manchester University Press.

McGivney, V. (1992). Women and vocational training: an overview. *Adults Learning*, 3,10.

Parsons, S. (1990). Feminist challenges to curriculum design. *Studies in the Education of Adults*, 22,1.

Robertson, R. (1992). *Globalisation*. London: Sage.

Sampson, E. (1993). *Celebrating the Other*. Hemel Hempstead: Harvester Wheatsheaf.

Thompson, J.L. (1983). *Learning Liberation*. London: Croom Helm.

Turner, B.S. (1993). Cruising America. In *Forget Baudrillard?* (eds. C. Rojek and B.S.Turner). London: Routledge.

Usher, R. and Edwards, R. (1994). *Postmodernism and Education: Different Voices, Different Worlds*. London: Routledge.

Weiler, K. (1991). Freire and a feminist pedagogy of difference. *Harvard Educational Review*, 61,4: 449-473.

Westwood, S. (1991). Constructing the future: a postmodern agenda for adult education. In *Radical Agendas? The Politics of Adult Education* (eds. S. Westwood and J.E. Thomas). Leicester: NIACE.

Williams, R. (1962). *The Long Revolution*. Harmondsworth: Penguin.

Preserving the Liberal Tradition in 'New Times'

Richard Taylor

Why should we want to preserve the liberal tradition? From all sides of the adult education world, and indeed in the wider context of the policy debate in education generally, the liberal tradition has been castigated. For the self-styled pragmatists of the Thatcherite right, the liberal tradition in education has stood both for the soft, pinko views of the public sector professionals and for the associated 'awkward squad' always theorising and criticising, and never getting down to the serious business of wealth creation. For many radicals — some socialists and feminists amongst them — the liberal tradition has embodied elitism and establishment values: at best a smokescreen and rationalisation for educational conformism, and at worst a means of social and cultural control.

It is my contention in this chapter that these views are untenable and that the liberal tradition, with all its faults, which I acknowledge and discuss below, should embody the kernel of radical adult education policy and practice for the future.

This is an opportune time to be discussing these issues. The old system of LEA adult education has been replaced very largely by FE provision as a result specifically of FE incorporation and, more generally, of the progressive emasculation of Local Authorities' powers by the Conservative government. (The focus in this chapter is upon university adult education but the same broad arguments apply, in my view, to the FE sector.) The changes in the university sector are no less fundamental. The Higher Education Funding Council's review of continuing education was triggered by the ending of the binary division and the consequent need to bring together in one coherent system the continuing education cultures and funding mechanisms of the 'old' and the 'new' universities (Duke and Taylor, 1994). There will be many consequences of the review but without doubt one of the most significant is the ending of non-accredited liberal adult education as a free-standing 'extra-mural' provision. The implications of these changes for the future structure and practice of university continuing education are returned to towards the end of the chapter.

The contention surrounding the liberal tradition is in part due to problems of definition. These are not merely definitional or semantic issues, however: the liberal tradition is an ideologically contested concept, and it also covers a wide spectrum of views and practices. To discuss its future we need first to look briefly at its past ideological structure.

There are certain characteristics which have been common to all forms of liberal adult education and are also inherent in what remains of the liberal ethos of higher education in general. Individualism, which of course lies at the heart of liberal ideology *per se*, has been central. The personal growth and development of the individual, through educational experience, has been seen as an *a priori* good, quite apart from the contingent benefits that such developed individuals might bring to the wider society.

Self-motivated, free individuals, fully aware of and involved with their fellows at a variety of levels, are seen as the cornerstone of the good society and the good life. Linked to this has been the concept of critical thinking. Liberal education should expose the individual learner to as wide a variety as possible of alternative views and analyses of the subject in question. The educational process should broaden understanding, encourage tolerance through an appreciation of others' world views, and, most importantly, develop the individual's critical faculties. Thus, within a fully-fledged liberal education context, all questions are open questions, all positions on all subjects are worthy of critical exploration and discussion, and all issues are subject only to the overriding test of rigorous intellectual analysis.

There is also a commitment to democratic practice in two particular respects: the educational process actively promotes an informed and questioning attitude and encourages, implicitly, involvement in both political and civil society: secondly, in the educational context itself, there is a commitment to a dialectical form of teaching, a dialogue between tutor and students and a 'negotiated' curriculum, a coming together of students' life experience and the tutor's academic knowledge (see E.P. Thompson, 1968).

All these have been generic characteristics of the liberal tradition. But there have been strongly divergent aspects too within the policy and practice of liberal adult education. The principal division has been between those who have seen liberal adult education as being primarily about individual self-development, unrelated — at least directly — to the social and political context. Albert Mansbridge was perhaps the most prominent advocate of such an approach. His credo centred on 'education for education's sake', combined with a passionate belief in the importance of enabling the mass of the working population to have access to the arts (high culture) and the academic and intellectual knowledge 'locked up' within the universities.

At the other end of the spectrum have been those who have had a 'social purpose' view of liberal adult education. Historically and ideologically this has been linked to the Labour Movement and its, maybe erstwhile, fundamental commitments to collectivism and to socialist change. Variants within this position have reflected the ideological differences between reformists and revolutionaries in the wider Labour Movement (see for example Miliband, 1973 and Coates, 1974), and the divisions and disputes in liberal adult education have been presented with a vehemence equal to that found in the political sphere. The division between the WEA and the National Council of Labour Colleges (NCLC) over the issue of the content and objectives of workers' education is probably the most prominent of the many historical examples of this conflict (Holford, 1994). What all these positions have had in common, however, is a belief that the primary purposes of adult education should be to act as the educational arm of the Labour Movement and to concentrate educational resources and commitment on the working class, however defined, and its emancipation. The emphases here, then, have been upon collective rather than individual approaches and upon broadly social science disciplinary areas.

The reformists — by far the majority in adult education as in the wider Labour Movement — have seen adult education within the parameters of democratic socialism (or Labourism as its critics have more often described it (Miliband, 1973; Coates, 1974; Nairn, 1961)). The concentration has been upon the practicalities of achieving reformist social change — applied economics, industrial law, industrial relations, elementary political theory and government, public administration, and so on. And the implicit ideological objectives have been to enculturate the working class (or its industrial vanguard) into the

Labour Movement and its world view. For the revolutionaries, whether Communist or libertarian Marxist of one sort or another, the objectives have been even more explicit: to counter bourgeois hegemony by giving working class adult students the opportunity to develop an alternative, Marxist, view of society. Even within this latter framework, the generic liberal values outlined earlier were usually adhered to: indeed, some of the finest exponents of liberal adult education in both its theory and its practice have been avowed Marxists (see E.P. Thompson, 1968 and Williams, 1962).

Until the 1980s, this liberal tradition in all its diversity was dominant in university adult education, as it was arguably in the whole university system. Thatcherite educational perspectives challenged this domi-nance but essentially they built upon pre-existing critiques of these liberal perspectives. As I noted at the beginning of this chapter, these critiques can be grouped conveniently under 'right' and 'left' perspec-tives. In some ways the ideas of the right are, atypically, more complex in this particular context. For those on the traditional 'old Tory' right, the elitism of the educational system was an essential part of a wider hierarchical and elitist social system. This had formed the tried and tested basis of the established British state for centuries. Far from being in need of egalitarian reform, it was precisely its elitist and hierarchical characteristics which provided its stability, quality and self-confidence (Hailsham, 1947; Beer, 1969). The role of the universities was essentially to reproduce 'renaissance men', gifted and educated amateurs, to administer the British state (and, until the late 1950s, the Empire). Universities were thus quintessentially about *liberal* education: techni-cal and professional competences could and should be learnt else-where. (Although even here there were contradictions, with some of the older professions, such as law and medicine, being regarded as wholly appropriate for university study.)

This approach is also inherently non-utilitarian. Kenneth Minogue (1973) has expressed this well:

> Academic inquiry is a manner of seeking to understand anything at all, a manner distinguished no doubt by its motives and preoccupa-tions, but distinguished above all by a quite different logic from that of practice. This means that there is a consistent difference in the kind of meaning that is found in academic discourse, by contrast with that found in the world at large. To ignore this difference, and to treat universities simply as institutions which provide educa-tional services for society is like treating a Ming vase as a cut-glass flower bowl: plausible, but crass.

For such elitist and 'academically pure' institutions to function properly there has to be a high degree of autonomy: this in turn entails non-interference by both the State and by private and public sector industry and commerce. As one analyst wrote, as long ago as 1975, the UGC seems 'more and more (to be) not the agent of the universities dealing with the State but, rather, the agent of the State vis-à-vis the universities' (MacRae, 1975). If this was true of the UGC in the 1970s, what price the Higher Education Funding Councils in the 1990s?

However, even before the trauma of Thatcherism and the destruction of the post-war welfare state consensus, this 'old Tory' view of education had been in decline. Ever since 1945, policy makers have been advocating a shift away from elitism and liberal emphases towards a strongly *utilitarian* model for all education, including Higher Education. This is not the place to enter into the detail of this debate. The main elements are familiar enough, however. The chronic long-term relative decline of the British economy is held widely to stem in part from a national lack of investment in training and technical competences. Moreover, the university system is held to have played a major part in establishing a status hierarchy — in this obsessively status conscious society — which places the arts, high culture, and the older professions at the pinnacle, and science and especially technology at the base. So, the argument goes, the needs of the State and the economy are, first, to shift the balance towards vocational, technologically and scientifically oriented programmes, and, secondly, to flatten and broaden the post-school structure so that far more people, both 18-21 year olds and older adults, have access to education and training. This is the backdrop to the current context of adult education, in both FE and universities: the rapid moves towards a mass higher education and the increasing blurring of the boundary between FE and HE; and the TEC-driven, vocationally oriented special funding initiatives which are combining with systemic reforms — CATS, modularisation, work-based and distance learning and so on — to change the whole nature of university education in Britain.

These utilitarian and vocational perspectives are ostensibly apolitical but tend implicitly to be strongly supportive of the established, capitalist, economic and social system (Taylor et al., 1985). From this perspective, the liberal tradition in adult education is a part of the old, anachronistic system that has been holding back the British economy. It needs to be replaced, it is argued, by an adult education that is both vocational — geared to the training and skills needs of the economy — *and populist* — making learning accessible to far larger numbers of adults the knowledge and skills that they need and want. There is little room, if any, here for the critical emphases of the liberal tradition: and none at all for either high culture or progressive social change perspectives.

From the Left, the critiques of the liberal tradition are equally vehement. At the risk of being over-schematic, these can be argued to fall into three sub-sets: socialist, community education, and feminist. For many socialists in adult education, especially those within the Marxist tradition, liberal adult education in the 1940s and 1950s was seen as a vehicle for Cold War orthodoxy (Fieldhouse, 1985). Ostensibly committed to liberal values — of objectivity, tolerance and so on — many senior figures in adult education, so it has been argued, were operating in fact from highly committed and exclusive, albeit implicit, Labourist perspectives (Fieldhouse, 1995). Just as, at some periods, the Communist Party's theoreticians dismissed social democratic political parties as class collaborators or, worse still, in the 1930s as social fascists, so socialist adult educators have often seen the WEA and university extra-mural departments as essentially, and by default, supportive of the *status quo*. Leaving aside the development of both professional and vocational provision in continuing education — which have certainly been amongst the main growth areas since 1945 — socialist adult educators have argued that liberal adult education has catered increasingly for a middle class and often dilettante student constituency. Moreover, the curriculum since the 1960s has seen a retreat from social science collectivist areas and a growth of subjects that are both participative and, more importantly in this context, localised and/or microcosmic in their concerns. They are often seemingly apolitical too or presented as if they were. Examples would include archaeology, local and regional history, laboratory and field-based science provision, and social psychology. To the extent that working class adult education has continued to be part of provision, it has concentrated increasingly upon 'technicist' education: collective bargaining aspects of industrial relations, health and safety, industrial law, and public administration and government (see McIlroy, 1988 and 1990; Holford, 1994).

These trends in adult education, it is argued, reflect wider social trends of political and social alienation, a retreat into consumerism and the private domestic sphere, and a culture dominated increasingly by material concerns (Taylor et al., 1985). Far from being a part of the solution to this depressing social situation, liberal adult education, it is argued, has been a part of the problem.

The community education movement in adult education had its modern roots in the 1960s, although its origins can be traced back well before that. It grew partly from the practice of radical social work, and particularly of community work, and partly from the theoretical and practical work and example of leading educators and activists in other countries — most notably perhaps Paulo Freire. Whilst essentially a part of the broadly socialist ideological framework, community education drew its inspiration from the realisation that neither the state nor any of its institutions, including the Labour Movement, was 'monolithic'. This was, in turn, a part of the dawning of Euro-communism and a more heterogeneous and diversified view of the structures of oppression. Although dismissed by both the 'Stalinists' of the old-style CP and the hard-liners of Trotskyism as bourgeois and dilettante, these perspectives quickly took hold in adult education as elsewhere and there was a rapid growth of interest in working with local people, on local issues, and in their localities (see Ward and Taylor (eds.), 1986). The critique of the liberal tradition here was that it was in all its central features bourgeois in both theory and practice. The curriculum of liberal adult education was derived from the academy and translated uncritically into the adult education context. The objectives and style of liberal adult education provision was either dilettante or, even more serious, removed from the real life struggles and experiences of working class people. The ethos of such provision was also essentially middle class: the seminar format, the 'expert tutor' imparting received wisdom, the institutional (university) location, and so on. Community education activists wanted to break through all this and create dynamic, issue-based, working class education which spoke to people's real felt needs and, through education, give communities both the confidence of knowledge leading to power, and its actuality. This involved challenging both traditional disciplinary boundaries and, more importantly, the epistemology of the academy. The various experimental work in the thirty or so years from the 1960s to the 1990s gives ample evidence of the energy and innovative abilities of both the professional community educators and of the communities they worked with and for (Ward and Taylor (eds.), 1986; Lovett, 1988).

Feminist perspectives also reject the liberal tradition with some vigour. Jane Thompson, for example, has argued that the liberal tradition has been not only elitist and essentially reactionary, but has also been permeated by patriarchal and sexist attitudes and practices (J. Thompson, 1980 and 1983).

One fundamental aspect of this challenge to liberal values is the assertion that homogeneous and committed adult education provision is wholly justified, indeed essential, when it takes place in the context of previously under-represented or 'disenfranchised' groups. Successive analyses have shown that universities at large, and even adult education, usually thought of as progressive in its practices, have been at best gender blind. In this context, the liberal tradition has been seen as part of the patriarchal system and, as such, inherently to be opposed by feminists. Of course, just as with the socialist left, feminism is divided into various 'factions' — liberal, socialist, radical and so on. But they all have in common, within the adult education context, a rejection of the liberal tradition, if not necessarily of all the values articulated on the radical end of the liberal spectrum.

In their different ways, these are all weighty criticisms. Equally important, the 'real world' context of the mid 1990s university is wholly unconducive to the liberal tradition. In the macrocosm, the rapid move to a mass system of FE and HE, with accompanying access missions and flexible study systems (modularisation et al.), sits uncomfortably with the traditional liberalism of the university system. Add to this the vocationalism which drives the government's access mission, and the liberal tradition seems to be a contemporary irrelevance. In the microcosm of adult education, the move to incorporation in FE and accreditation in HE — again coupled with the increasing vocationalism in both sectors — would seem to spell the end of the century-old liberal tradition.

At the heart of this contemporary discussion must be the issue of access and accessibility (see Yeo, 1991). At one level, the whole history of university adult education, and arguably adult education in its entirety, has been concerned with trying to obtain some limited access into a closed, elitist system for the large majority of the population which has been excluded. University Extension, the WEA, the Joint Tutorial classes structure, the post-war extra-mural departments and so on, were all designed to provide educational opportunities separate from the mainstream, 'outside the walls' of the institutional complex which served the needs of the elite. Honourable and valuable though this tradition has been, it has always been by definition marginal to the mainstream.

With the coming of mass further and higher education, this marginality is potentially at an end: 'from margins to mainstream' indeed! Of course, there are dangers for the mainstream system to confront. Government is determined not only to increase the vocational and market orientation of both FE and HE, it is also intent on driving down unit costs as the numbers and thus the bottom line, total costs of the system increase. There are real issues here of quality, drop-out, and ultimately the value placed by society at large upon a university or FE award.

But there is also the crucial issue of 'Access to what?' The historic objectives of the liberal tradition of adult education — to open up the world of learning, knowledge, and, some added, therefore power and the ability to use education for progressive change — can now be achieved potentially by very large numbers of the population through the mainstream system. In the medium term, therefore, there is only a very limited need for separate special provision for under-repre- sented groups. (Hence there is logical appeal, other political things being equal — which of course they are not — in the Funding Council's decision in 1994 to earmark a special but small fund for 'access and disadvantaged' adult education work.) However, whereas in the past it has been assumed with little if any discussion, save amongst Marx- ists, and latterly feminists, that access to the *existing* provision of universities and other educational institutions was the objective, this cannot now be taken for granted.

The burden of the discussion earlier about current trends in univer- sities was that they were becoming not only mass institutions but that their *raison d'etre* and consequently their curricular norms (and their research norms too, though this is not so relevant to this discussion), were becoming increasingly influenced by market and individualistic criteria. This should not be over-emphasised: it is true that the liberal ethos survives battered but largely intact in most universities. Never- theless, it is undeniable that the combination of the moves towards mass education, at cheaper unit cost, and with a stronger market orientation, has produced a marked and accelerating change in univer- sity culture.

In a society where individualism, personal advancement and wealth creation are more dominant and explicit motivations than ever before, will greater access to HE result 'merely' in increased upward social mobility for significant numbers of people? And, if it does, will this be necessarily a bad thing? (After all, it is ethically dubious, to say the least, for those of us with professional careers and all that goes with that, to denigrate individual, material progress through educational opportu- nity.) Nevertheless, this issue becomes particularly acute, especially for those adult educators who view the liberal tradition as essentially concerned with collective social purpose, when the sharp decline of the socialist project is taken into account. In the past, the point of identifi- cation was the Labour Movement, or some particular element within it (the CP for example). That has now largely disappeared. Most people in education, and virtually everyone in adult education (Fieldhouse, 1993), would welcome the return of a Labour government: but few would claim that this will represent, at least in the foreseeable future, the basis for fundamental socialist change. The Labour Party has long ceased to be, as Ralph Miliband pointed out some years ago, a reformist party and has become instead a party of, very modest, social reform (Miliband, 1973 and 1977).

Access, and by association the liberal tradition, is thus no longer linked clearly to a wider ideological and political formation. This is the other sense of the 'New Times' in which we now live. The post-modern, post-industrial and — maybe — post-ideological era is not an intellectually comfortable place to be. Much of the familiar ideological and intellectual furniture has moved or indeed disappeared. And, in the organisational microcosm of university continuing education, the change to a mainstreamed, accredited system will bring liberal adult education right into the heart of the system.

This change is fundamental. It does mean, in effect, the end of the separate liberal tradition of adult education. Probably, there will be no more charismatic extra-mural stars like E.P. Thompson and Williams. More importantly, both the freedom to construct curricula to suit the needs and aspirations of particular adult groups will be curtailed, and the sense of an adult education movement will decline, or, maybe, just change its nature. Accreditation also means, by definition, that adult education provision will become assessed, and integrated into the credentialling and QA processes of the wider institution. All these aspects of accreditation, despite the potential advantages, are distasteful for many adult educators and indeed for many adult students. Undoubtedly, these changes signify the end of an era.

However, the fact of accreditation does not of itself negate the values and practices of the radical, social purpose liberal tradition. There is every reason for CE practitioners to seize the moment on behalf of the potential mass of previously excluded people. With modular structures, and increasing emphases on recruiting more non-standard students — work-based learning initiatives, for example — all manner of innovation is possible. Interdisciplinary programmes, for example, can be designed to meet the needs of particular groups; more flexible and appropriate assessment methods can be devised as part of the learning process rather than separate from it; and a variety of awards, both competency-based such as NVQ 4 and 5 and credit-based below degree level such as Certificate and Diploma, can be introduced.

But, for all these desirable developments to be articulated properly and progressively, it is now more important than ever, that the values and practices of the liberal tradition are maintained and extended.

Despite the elitism, sexism and the rest, the old university system did encompass some critical elements of the liberal approach: the quest for knowledge for its own sake, the inculcation of critical thinking, and the commitment to intellectual openness and tolerance, were amongst them. All these, and many other, attributes of the university system are under threat for a combination of organisational, ideological, and financial reasons.

In the past, the 'liberal tradition debate' was confined largely to the separate world of adult education. It was important to us professionally in the trade but, to be frank, it was of relatively little interest to the university world at large. Now, for the first time, and for a combination of reasons bad as well as good, *continuing education* concerns are at the heart of the *universities'* agenda. There is now the opportunity for the progressive perspectives and practices of CE to 'colonise the mainstream'. To preserve the radical social purpose liberal tradition, and the values it embodies, will require some hard re-formulations and the jettisoning of much bad practice (see Holloway, 1994). But the kernel of the liberal tradition — its commitment to democratic practice, to critical thinking, and to intellectual openness and tolerance — has the opportunity to make a profound impact on the newly accessible and mass higher education system that is emerging. A revitalised liberal tradition in adult — and further and higher — education also has the role, in my view, of contributing to wider social and political change and of resurrecting in changed form its connections with democratic socialist politics. But that is tomorrow's possible agenda: for the present it will be hard enough, but important, to ensure that a reformed and dynamic liberal tradition plays its role at the centre of continuing education policy and practice in the new world of mass higher education.

References

Beer, S.H. (1969). *Modern British Politics*. Faber and Faber.

Coates, D. (1974). *The Labour Party and the Struggle for Socialism*. Cambridge University Press.

Duke, C. and Taylor, R. (1994). The HEFCE review and the funding of continuing education. *Studies in the Education of Adults*, 26.1, 86-94.

Fieldhouse, R. (1985). *Adult Education and the Cold War: Liberal Values Under Siege 1946-51.* University of Leeds Press.

Fieldhouse, R. (1993). *Optimism and Joyful Irreverence.* NIACE.

Fieldhouse, R. (1995). Sidney Raybould, Fred Sedgwick and the early department. In *Fifty Years of Continuing Education at the University of Leeds* (ed. R. Taylor). University of Leeds Press.

Hailsham, (Lord) (1947). *The Case for Conservatism.* Penguin Books.

Holford, J. (1994). *Union Education in Britain.* Department of Adult Education, University of Nottingham.

Holloway, G. (ed.) (1994). *All Change! Accreditation as a Challenge to Liberal Adult Education.* Centre for Continuing Education, University of Sussex.

Lovett, T. (ed.) (1988). *Radical Approaches to Adult Education: a Reader.* Routledge.

MacRae, D. (1975). The British position. In *Universities in the Western World,* (ed. P. Seabury). Collier Macmillan.

McIlroy, J. (1988). Storm and stress: the Trades Union Congress and university adult education 1964-1974. *Studies in the Education of Adults,* 20.1, 60-73.

McIlroy, J. (1990). Trade union education for a change. In *The Search for Enlightenment : The Working Class and Adult Education in the Twentieth Century* (ed. B. Simon). Lawrence and Wishart.

Miliband, R. (1973). *Parliamentary Socialism* (second edition). Merlin Press.

Miliband, R. (1977). *Marxism and Politics.* Oxford University Press.

Minogue, K. (1973). *The Concept of a University.* Weidenfeld and Nicolson.

Nairn, T. (1961). The Nature of the Labour Party. In *Towards Socialism* (eds. T. Nairn and P. Anderson). New Left Books.

Taylor, R., Rockhill, K. and Fieldhouse, R. (1985). *University Adult Education in England and the USA: A Reappraisal of the Liberal Tradition.* Croom Helm.

Thompson, E.P. (1968). Education and Experience. *Fifth Mansbridge Memorial Lecture.* University of Leeds Press.

Thompson, J. (ed.) (1980). *Adult Education for a Change.* Hutchinson.

Thompson, J. (1983). *Learning Liberation.* Croom Helm.

Ward, K. and Taylor, R. (eds.) (1986). *Adult Education and the Working Class: Education for the Missing Millions.* Croom Helm.

Williams, R. (1962). *The Long Revolution.* Penguin.

Yeo, S. (1991). Access: 'What and Whither, When and How'. *Fourteenth Albert Mansbridge Memorial Lecture.* University of Leeds Press.

The Great Tradition — A Personal Reflection

Jane L. Thompson

In a world in which many adult education workers either 'mourn the passing' or 'do not remember' much about the heady days (*sic*) of adult education before the Thatcher-Major onslaught — it seems important, in the context of a collection like this, to remind ourselves about some of the limitations of the so called 'Great Tradition', in case a kind of ritual eulogy to the words and wisdom of Harold Wiltshire et al. serves to obscure or romanticise a far from perfect past.

My reflections are not those of an academic theorist, concerned about the nature and meaning of liberal adult education in its philosophical context, so much as the experience and analysis of one whose purpose and practice as an adult educator has been developed and clarified in the context of profound irritation with the liberal tradition and growing opposition to the new vocationalism which has largely replaced it.

Having lived through a period of considerable economic and social restructuring — I am writing in October 1994 — and of changes which have not simply affected education but are epitomised in what is often referred to as a 'paradigm shift' in both the thinking and practice of education, there is again a feeling of change in the air. Not particularly because there is much to be optimistic about in the educational policy statements emanating from New Labour or the recommendations of the Commission for Social Justice but more because the almost 'absolute' and 'divine right to rule' assumed by successive Tory governments in recent years, and translated into a near totalitarian political orthodoxy in the eighties by the relentlessness of Thatcherism, has at last begun to crumble. Despite the ongoing efforts of the Tory Right to place a further stretch of 'clear blue water' between themselves and any likely competition for the middle ground in British politics, the momentum which a few years ago seemed to be unstoppable, is now in a state of collapse. Even in its own terms — to do with traditional values, rewarding individual initiative, self-styled occupation of the high moral ground and business enterprise, the Thatcher legacy is becoming tainted and less effective than it once was. There is space around the edges once again, and even in the more traditional heartlands, for mobilising effective opposition (Thompson, 1993).

As politicians begin to re-group, and new arrangements are invented to make sense of national and international responses to post-communism, late capitalism and globalisation — the cultural and ideological role of education as a crucial and contested site of struggle needs to be understood, debated and practised with the conviction that, what each of us is able to do, either contributes to or detracts from our visions of what might happen next, at this important moment of historical change. The recognition of the relationship between education and activism expressed by Paulo Freire in *Pedagogy of the Oppressed* is still as relevant today:

> Education either functions as an instrument which is used to facilitate the integration of generations into the logic of the present system and bring about conformity to it, or it becomes 'the practice of freedom', the means by which men and women deal critically with reality and discover how to participate in the transformation of their world.

The liberal tradition in adult education, sometimes referred to as the Great Tradition, also had its philosophy and visions, as others in this collection will explain. Measured against the rather pragmatic, materialistic, and cost effective criteria of market derived and market driven preoccupations of recent years, it has become commonplace, in the fringe meetings of local gatherings and national conferences, to hear beleaguered and nostalgic expressions of regret from those old enough to remember a time before Thatcher, when the language of 'learning for its own sake', 'learning for pleasure' and 'responding to students' needs' was part of the everyday understanding of liberal adult education workers.

Bombarded more recently on all sides by funding-related accreditation schemes, marketing strategies, performance indicators, quality control requirements and competency criteria — a new language has been developed which has made it increasingly more difficult to talk about students and adult learners as distinct from customers and unit costs; to talk about the meaning and purpose of education as distinct from strategic plans and mission statements; to talk about the nature of the curriculum and appropriate teaching methods as distinct from modularisation and appraisal mechanisms; to talk about equal opportunities as distinct from student numbers; to talk about thinking and questioning as distinct from measuring and monitoring. As the very concept of 'adult education' disappears from official descriptions of educational policy, the practice of adult education also becomes increasingly difficult to distinguish and sustain. Keith Jackson (1995) reminds us about the senior civil servant's telling paraphrase of Thatcher's own apocryphal vision of society, 'there is no such thing as adult education today, only adults attending classes'.

In this kind of context, there are those who are nostalgic for a time when the so-called 'pleasure' and 'confidence', alleged to derive from flower arranging and cake decorating classes, often led to a life transformed by adult education and progression to more challenging academic experiences was held to be commonplace. It was a time when 'the best that has been thought and said' and which was thought to be enshrined in university based knowledge, was extended beyond the boundaries of the academy to those 'in the community' through extramural and voluntary body provision, so they could also experience 'high status' knowledge, with its alleged capacity to cultivate individual enlightenment, civilisation, and personal fulfilment in 'the true spirit' of a democratic society. These justifications and idealisations now have an immensely 'faded former era' feel about them, but they linger in apparent contrast to the current preoccupations with credit accumulation and transfer schemes, operating like banks in an inflationary economy, to print currency like confetti, and create qualifications that are hardly worth the paper they are printed on, except as a major diversion from a different kind of analysis about what is really going on.

My purpose here is not to de-construct the new educational language and institutional changes which so many former liberals, and indeed socialists, in adult education have seemingly been eager to adopt, as an indication of their recognition of 'realism' during the Thatcher and Major years, except to note that it has happened (Thompson, 1993). However I suggest that this shift in paradigm, this systematic accommodation to the language and policies of the New

Right has found those in adult education to be much more amenable, on the whole, to its logic and demands than school teachers have been prepared to be.

If the shifts in emphasis which have been brought about in adult and continuing education are viewed in the general context of New Right attempts to remake all manner of public services, including the health service and social services, into business enterprises, governed by the so-called logic of the market; and to undermine potential sources of considered opposition like local authorities and trade unions; and to reduce the opportunities for democratic accountability in favour of various unaccountable quangos, leaving little to choose between the organisation and ethos of privatised and regulatory bodies like Oftel (in relation to British Telecom) and Ofsted (in relation to education); then the energetic and enthusiastic acceptance of government directives by adult educators concerned to engage *more* students in *less* face to face teaching and critical thinking, in the name of modularisation, 'flexible learning', 'self directed study' and dubious academic and vocational qualifications, is hardly the radical collective response to these measures we might have hoped for.

The extent and enthusiasm of the response by adult education workers to what amounts to a serious attack on the potentially radical and critical role of adult education both to inform and assist in the process of democratic participation, social liberation, and political transformation, is in my view a direct consequence of the previous enthusiasm of adult education workers for the liberal tradition. In other words, the Great Tradition as it developed, and as it was provided in the heady days before Thatcher, helped to *lay the foundations* and *prepare the way* for what was then to be an unseemly rush to the Right, which through a series of decisive cuts and government policy directives, soon proceeded to relegate its insignificance to history.

My first experience of adult education happened in Hull, in a working class comprehensive school, in the early 1970s. The school was a concrete and glass monstrosity a short bus ride from where I grew up before going to university. It was built on the remains of a bombsite, in the only square space of unoccupied land between factories and terrace houses, packed cheek by jowl between the docks and a maximum security prison. But it was 1970. I joined the women's liberation group (whatever happened to liberation?) with Lily Bilocca to relate the emergence of second wave feminism to the class struggle, and in particular the campaign led by fishermen's wives to get radio systems installed on trawlers in a year when ships and men were lost without trace in the perilous fishing grounds off Iceland. As a group we clubbed together to send one of our members to the first National Women's Liberation conference at Ruskin College in February and knew, when she returned, that we were in some sense 'making history'.

During the day I introduced working class kids destined for the trawlers, Reckitt and Colemans and the Metal Box factory to the study of sociology, just as O and A levels in the subject were being invented and whilst sociology was still considerably identified with the New Left and student politics of the late 60s.

These were 'the days of miracles and wonder' when IMG, Civil Rights, Anti Vietnam War demonstrations and the re-emergence of feminism were formative influences on a generation of first generation recruits into 'lesser professional' jobs as cultural workers. When left wing intellectuals joined with the members of the working class in community education and development projects to try to make the state more accountable to the concerns of working class people in the belief that information, agitation and collaboration in a democratic society was what led to social change.

At night in the comprehensive school I worked with the tutor organiser for the WEA to provide a range of evening meetings, political workshops, short courses and conferences for local people, on issues to do with housing rights, education, community action campaigns and economic issues. Together we produced a newspaper; we ran a conference about equal opportunities in education in the days when the abolition of streaming and mixed ability teaching were signs of progress; and got parents involved in public planning meetings, oral history projects and worker-writer groups. He was said to be a communist by his colleagues. I had no idea that what we were doing was progressive in conventional adult education circles.

By the time I was appointed to the Adult Education Department at Southampton University, as Lecturer in Community Education, I had considerable understanding, from my own background and my previous work, about the relationship between social class, the mal-distribution of power and resources in society, and the role of adult education as a necessary provider of the kind of learning identified by Richard Johnson (1979) in earlier times as 'really useful knowledge'. In the nineteenth century, in the pages of the Poor Man's Guardian (1832), this meant knowledge that sought to make sense of the causes of hardship and oppression in working class people's lives:

...to enable men to judge correctly of the real causes of misery and distress so prevalent ... to consider what remedies will prove most effectual in removing the causes of those evils so that the moral and political influence of the people may be united for the purpose of supporting such measures as are really calculated to improve their condition.

As myself and others have argued frequently elsewhere, and most recently in *Adult Learning, Critical Intelligence and Social Change* (Mayo and Thompson, eds., 1995), this concept remains crucial in contemporary circumstances because it implies knowledge which connects the cultural with the intellectual and the practical, makes no crude distinctions between what is vocational and non-vocational, and depends for its curriculum on the material concerns and political interests of those for whom education cannot be seen as the luxury of leisure or progression, but must help to make sense of intolerable circumstances with a view to changing them.

Three years prior to my appointment at Southampton, the Russell Report had argued that there was a strong case for expanding adult education provision to 'the socially and culturally deprived, living in urban areas' which would often have an 'experimental and informal character'. The Russell Report was part of the same momentum which produced a decade of reports into town planning (Skeffington), primary education (Plowden), the personal social services (Seebohm) etc., and which were responding to perceived failures in the structures and processes of the welfare state. Russell shared with these other reports the basic assumption that the political economy of the welfare state was not itself problematic. As Jackson (1995) points out:

... there was no break with the consensus which had dominated public policy since the 1940s, namely that the fundamental problems of a capitalist political economy had been resolved by a balance of class forces, with the state acting as a means of regulating the economy in order to ensure full employment and social justice. In seeking to tidy up the edges of the welfare state none of the reports considered that the problems they were addressing might be manifestations of a more fundamental crisis in the political economy.

The Russell Report in its turn recommended a variety of 'experimental' and interventionist gestures which gave rise to a spate of community adult education projects in the decade which followed. Such was the Southampton Department's New Communities Project (Fordham et al., 1979) in the hinterland of Portsmouth and which initiative I was appointed to develop.

In practice I was unprepared for how pervasively the liberal assumptions of the Great Tradition — inherent in the working practices of the Department, in which key individuals had learned their trade in Nottingham at the feet of Harold Wiltshire — had shaped the formulation and assessment of what the research revealed. Nowhere in the published findings of the research, or in the plans for the future, was there any significant analysis of class or gender, or any recognition that what could be counted on as education in the project was being used as a diversion, a form of 'second rate' knowledge, concerned as one resident put it to 'keep the buggers happy', and justified in terms of being 'less threatening'. It was clearly just another form of social control rather than a means of personal and collective liberation which paid serious attention to the serious circumstances in which many in the community were forced to live. Theoretical references to the works of Illich and Friere remained theoretical and locked into the safety of foreign contexts which were sufficiently removed from the day to day reality of downtown Southampton and Portsmouth in the middle seventies to be found interesting but not applicable.

I think my appointment was generally viewed by those who made it as something of a mistake judging by the amount of resistance I subsequently encountered to the deployment of a Marxist, and increasingly, a feminist analysis. In the wake of publications I was associated with, like *Adult Education For a Change* and *Learning Liberation*, the full weight of the Department's liberal tradition rallied behind notions of 'educational neutrality', 'academic objectivity', the 'tutorial tradition' and a highly particular (i.e. dead, white, male, middle class and european) selection of knowledge and culture confirmed as 'truth'.

I recount this now not to pick away at old scars or to settle old scores but as an illustration of one of the most significant limitations of the liberal tradition — its profound resistance to any form of structural or material explanations of social and educational inequality or educational elitism. Because it was alleged that 'access to adult education' was 'open to all', and because it was assumed that any failure on the part of potential students to participate was either to do with their cultural deficiency (Thompson, 1980) or inefficient advertising and recruitment procedures on the part of institutions (Rogers, 1973; Newman, 1979), the cultural control of adult education by dominant forms of knowledge and ideology, and its appropriation by those with already huge amounts of middle class cultural capital, was taken for granted.

There were of course voices of dissent — many of those who contributed to *Adult Education for a Change*, for example, and who worked in grim urban neighbourhoods, trade union meeting places and community projects — trying to relate the acquisition of 'really useful knowledge' and critical intelligence to intellectual understanding and collective social action. They worked in the kind of contexts and with the kind of students which those enmeshed in the Great Tradition rarely encountered, except as occasional and idiosyncratic individuals who defied all sociological generalisations and occasionally found their way into tutorial classes as token workers.

The liberal tradition, of course, did not recognise as a problem the middle class bias of the student body, or the implicitly elitist assumptions built into the selection and delivery of the curriculum. Nor did it recognise until it was pointed out by commentators like Nell Keddie (1980) and myself how individualistic and selective were its perspectives. The fact that large numbers of organisers and tutors at university level were men and large numbers of students were women went largely unnoticed until Keddie pointed to the ways in which the organisation and curriculum of liberal adult education operated according to an ideology of individualism which acted to conform women students particularly to the logic of the status quo. In *Learning Liberation* I commented on the extent to which the liberal tradition reflected the selection of knowledge and teaching methods established historically by white middle class men and which in the process ignored or silenced the material, gender and cultural concerns of working class people, women and ethnic minority groups. Despite sweeping claims laid to universal qualities of reason, truth, enlightenment and democracy, the voices of the powerless, including working class and black people, the unemployed, lesbians and gay men and women speaking in their own right were largely missing from the classrooms of the Great Tradition.

Throughout the 1970s and 1980s it was not tutorial classes in 'Chaucer and his Times' or 'Medieval Castles' which registered the significance of adult education as an activity worth defending when the cuts began. Although defined as 'marginal' it was the work done by people like Keith Jackson (1974) and Martin Yarnit in Liverpool and Tom Lovett (1975) in Northern Ireland which sought to re-constitute the resources of the Great Tradition, as symbolic of a particular kind of intellectual property which needed to be socialised and radicalised and redistributed in more appropriate and democratic forms to those who were excluded from its privileges — using very similar kinds of arguments to those which influenced the establishment of Ruskin College and the Labour College Movement (Brown, 1980). The same arguments characterised the nineteenth century radical tradition, seeking the kind of knowledge that would help to 'get us out of our present troubles' (Poor Man's Guardian, 1934): the kind of knowledge that was related to the material, social, political and cultural conditions of working class life, which could provide insight and understanding, which could provide a critical analysis of systems of oppression privilege and power and which might assist people in their collective efforts to make changes. It was this kind of knowledge and purpose which fitted very well with trade union education, with feminist education, with community action, with equal opportunities initiatives and with anti-racist strategies in the 70s and 80s (O'Rourke, 1995) — all of which offered contemporary reincarnations of traditional radical concerns to treat education as a tool of liberation rather than a means of elitist reproduction and social control.

When the New Right arrived the Great Tradition was ill prepared to make any other response except capitulation. Living comfortably on the periphery of university life for many years, extra-mural departments enjoyed all the privileges of academic life and avoided most of the internal rivalries. Whilst some academics from intra-mural departments looked down on extra-mural departments as being 'not quite scholarly enough', and some extra-mural academics looked down on WEA tutors as being 'not quite scholarly enough', and all of them looked down on LEA provision as dealing in hobbies and remedial education, the New Right arrived to produce the inevitable shake up. When research profiles and funding, profit and cost efficiency became the order of the day, adult education departments became vulnerable. The long-standing complacency and elitism of the Great Tradition was in itself found wanting by comparison to the more aggressive machismo of intra-mural centres of alleged excellence. Once deficit funding was replaced by financial targets, the last vestiges of pretence about 'learning for its own sake' and knowledge that constituted 'the best which had been thought and said' were jettisoned in the search for new markets — any markets — and for commodities that could be packaged and sold in ways that would provide income (see Jackson, 1995).

Continuing education sought to distance itself from adult education and the liberal tradition and took on a very different meaning and remit from that of 'life long learning'. In universities up and down the land continuing education became synonymous with award bearing qualifications and with those professions and individuals who could pay to have themselves 'up-graded', 'refreshed' and 'requalified'. Management training, frequently related to specific vocational areas, became a minor empire. Such initiatives and franchise deals with lower status institutions to promote access courses sought to supply increasing numbers of 'non traditional students' to comply with government directives and the necessary 'bums on seats' to meet funding requirements. In the process, worthy but financially unviable provision was scrapped, as was labour-intensive, non-profit-making, troublesome and contentious work, promoted by those whose institutional loyalty (as distinct from loyalty to working class and disempowered communities) and conversion to 'new realism' could not be guaranteed.

In 1986, three weeks into a new term of a year long 'Second Chance' programme for working class women, most of whom were single parents and living on benefits in downtown Southampton, the University Department responsible for its funding decided, without any consultation, to close down the crèche, sack part-time tutors and insist that all course fees be found in full. It took a well attended demonstration and a national press campaign to shame the Department into restoring its financial commitment to the course but not without the organising tutor, who was alleged to have brainwashed around 200 women and children into demonstrating on behalf of women's education, from being disciplined for 'professional disloyalty' to the University (Taking Liberties Collective, 1989).

Of course the Great Tradition, like many other relics of former, more consensual times, like trade union politics and local council democracy, was 'on the run' from the New Right. But as a measure of its support in academia and in the wider community, very little in the way of demonstrations and national press campaigns were mounted in its support. Whatever 'learning' it had helped to provide 'for pleasure' or 'for its own sake' across the years, it had not been sufficient to turn an essentially individualistic uncommitted student body into a vociferous movement prepared to speak out in its defence. And when the New Right shifted the goal posts to require more 'non traditional' students, credit transfer schemes, accreditation of prior learning, access courses and modularisation — the new directives were embraced with a mixture of cooperation and resignation.

A new 'enthusiasm' was generated for mature, working class, black and women students, whose educational interests and rights, ten years previously, it had seemed like a Marxist\communist\radical feminist heresy to promote. But also resignation because, short of taking early retirement, there seemed to be little other alternative but to go along with the new directives. Those of us who had spent many years arguing for access to the opportunities of university education for those groups of students who were conventionally excluded, and for the transformation of the culture and curriculum of university education to recognise student diversity — especially in terms of class, 'race' and gender (Thompson, 1987) — knew that the new access industry was more about 'jobs for the boys' and about quantity rather than quality (Taking Liberties Collective, 1989). And that schemes concerned with credit accumulation and modularisation only made sense if you viewed education as a commodity to be collected like green shield stamps — as quickly and as mechanistically as possible — in case you should take time to think, or engage in critical analysis, or begin to make the kind of connections with others which might lead to collective action for social change.

The price paid for 'upgrading' former polytechnics to universities and spreading modularisation like wildfire has been to reduce the number of hours in which a student can expect to be taught; increase the size of groups to effectively eliminate any other teaching method except lectures; and remove all but tokenistic responsibility for student growth and emotional development, by eliminating the pastoral and personal tutor function, and splintering the possibility of a 'learning community' into a postmodernist nightmare of atomised and unrelated fragments. As 'self directed study' methods replace human contact, and human teaching gives way to computer technology, the potential for student alienation and drop out can only increase. Despite, and some would say because of, the contradiction which is everywhere revered as 'quality control' and 'total quality management'.

As fewer and fewer teachers teach more and more people, it seems increasingly probable that output might exceed demand. In such circumstances the qualifications being gained become correspondingly irrelevant and obsolete, not to mention the notable absence of significant opportunities gained as a consequence of simply surviving the process. In such circumstances it feels possible to explain the country's current obsession with the National Lottery as some kind of metaphor which appears to provide about as realistic an assessment of 'changing one's life' as any other! Meanwhile, the recognition by the rich and famous of the allegation that the University of Huddersfield, for example, can't possibly be regarded as the same as the University of Oxford, or even Warwick, has encouraged the setting up of a new super league of around twelve ancient and aspiring universities, which will pay their staff more and charge additional fees, to promote their exclusive excellence and superiority, as the market again rises to the challenge of 'flexible specialisation' as distinct from mass production.

Writing in *Adults Learning* in October 1993, in response to my appeal to those who were 'still left' and working to offer alternatives to New Right orthodoxy in adult and continuing education, Malcolm Barry praised others like himself who had 'kept their heads down' and worked 'on the inside' to make the best of what was possible. His caricature of those still operating in the radical tradition was of latter day loonies now reafflicted with political correctness, who had persuaded no one but themselves about the importance of the class struggle or women's liberation, and who had totally misjudged the mood of the working class and their obvious enthusiasm for the promises of increased affluence under the Tories.

Of course it was not simply the socialist visions of the radical tradition which got steam rollered by the relentless rush to the right during the 1980s and early 90s. The GLC and ILEA could not prevent themselves being disbanded. Trade unions floundered as restrictive legislation stripped them of their powers and room to manoeuvre. Local authorities were penalised for exercising local democratic mandates to contradict government directives, until they too were left in the position of administering centralised policies which many of them did not like but were powerless to prevent. Quangos replaced democratically elected and publicly accountable bodies. Citizens became clients, purchasing services from an increasingly privatised 'public' sector with charters to identify their rights as consumers — though not to guarantee them. Wage councils were abolished. The social chapter wasn't signed. The welfare state was systematically restructured. Compulsory Competitive Tendering in the public sector and the introduction of new contracts in the further education sector all helped to reduce wages, increase working hours, deskill workers, and further discipline an already demoralised workforce. De-regulation in industry, in the guise of removing unnecessary red tape conspired, with everything else, to turn Britain into one of the lowest low wage, long hours economies in Europe. I could go on.

In the face of this kind of onslaught it is not surprising that the Great Tradition gave in and that the radical tradition in adult education did not, by itself, save the day. But what is surprising, and well worth celebrating, is that despite an extremely cold climate for the left in recent years, and despite widespread accommodation to the right by liberals in education, the radical tradition has survived. John McIlroy (1995) makes the point very well. He reminds those like Barry (1993) who have boasted about 'keeping their heads down', and who have consigned the radical tradition to stereotype, that quite a lot of us are still around. We haven't 'kept our heads down' but we have continued to work against the grain in a committed way, according to principle, and with principles, in the pursuit of principles — without being excluded. The publication of *Adult Learning, Critical Intelligence and Social Change* in 1995 is in itself a testimony to the continuing presence of the radical tradition at the cutting edge of adult education theory and practice. Just as it always was. And in ways which have survived the Thatcher and Major years. Offering alternative analyses, evidence and proposals about how, in the current context, we continue to pursue the goals of radical praxis and critical intelligence, concerned to raise consciousness and provide tools for liberation in anticipation of the 'practice of freedom' which Friere (1972) talked about, and with which 'men and women can deal creatively with reality and discover how to participate in the transformation of their world'.

References

Barry, M. (1993). Learning, humility and honesty! *Adults Learning*, October 1993.

Brown, G. (1980). Independence and incorporation: the Labour College movement and the Workers Education Association before the second world war. In *Adult Education for a Change* (ed. J. Thompson). Hutchinson.

Fordham, P., Poulton G. and Randle, L. (eds.) (1979). *Learning Networks in Adult Education: Non-Formal Education on a Housing Estate*. R.K.P.

Freire, P. (1972). *Pedagogy of the Oppressed*. Harmondsworth, Penguin.

Jackson, K. (1974). Adult education and the social action. In *Community Work One* (eds. Jones, D. and M. Mayo). R.K.P.

Jackson, K. (1995). Popular education and the state: a new look at the community debate. In *Adult Learning, Critical Intelligence and Social Change* (eds. M. Mayo, M. and J. Thompson). NIACE.

Johnson, R. (1979). Really useful knowledge: radical education and working class culture 1790-1848. In *Working Class Culture: Studies in History and Theory* (eds. J. Clarke, C. Critcher, R. and Johnson). Hutchinson.

Keddie, N. (1980). Adult education — an ideology of individualism. In *Adult Education for a Change* (ed. J. Thompson). Hutchinson.

Lovett, T. (1975). *Adult Education, Community Development and the Working Class*. Ward Lock.

Mayo, M. and Thompson, J. (eds.) (1995). *Adult Learning, Critical Intelligence and Social Change*. NIACE.

McIlroy, J. (1995). Preface. In *Adult Learning, Critical Intelligence and Social Change* (eds. M. Mayo and J. Thompson). NIACE.

Newman, M. (1975). *Poor Cousin: A Study of Adult Education*. Allen and Unwin.

O'Rourke, R. (1995). All equal now? In *Adult Learning, Critical Intelligence and Social Change* (eds. M. Mayo, M. and J. Thompson). NIACE.

Poor Man's Guardian (March 1832). No. 35.

Poor Man's Guardian (September 1834). No. 137.

Rogers, J. (1977). *Adults Learning* (2nd edition). Oxford University Press.

Taking Liberties Collective (1989). *Learning the Hard Way: Women's Oppression in Men's Education*. Macmillan.

Thompson, J. (1980). Adult education and the disadvantaged. In *Adult Education for a Change* (ed. J. Thompson). Hutchinson.

Thompson, J. (ed.) (1980). *Adult Education for a Change*. Hutchinson.

Thompson, J. (1983). *Learning Liberation: Women's Response to Men's Education*. Croom Helm.

Thompson, J. (1987). The cost and value of higher education to working class women. In *Oxford and Working Class Education* (ed. S. Harrop). Department of Adult Education, University of Nottingham.

Thompson, J. (1993). Learning, liberation and maturity. *Adults Learning*, vol. 4, no. 9.

From The Great Tradition to NVQs
Universities and Trade Union Education at *Fin de Siecle*

John McIlroy

And is it not important that the values and purposes of the great tradition, though developed in another age, should be carried over into this? They will be against the grain but is that not their value?

Harold Wiltshire (1956)

Trade unions, as John Kenneth Galbraith eloquently urged, are one of the great civilising influences of capitalism. Because of their importance as arenas of working class activity and agents of social change they have been of continuing interest to university adult educators operating from a variety of ideological perspectives within a broad tradition of social reform. That tradition which viewed the Labour movement as central to a coalition for progressive social change has since the 1970s been under severe siege. University adult education has been progressively restructured in the mould of vocational training and education for profitable leisure. Its clientele is increasingly the already educated pursuing self development, the techniques of cultural appreciation, the skills of technology and self-therapy, the expertise required by the discerning consumer and the productive human resource. It has been reinvented configured by the new self interested, individualism, enterprise and consumer culture, as a private want resourced through the market rather than a public good. Its links with trade unions have decreased significantly. The Labour movement itself of course has faced even greater attrition, decline, and loss of sense of social mission.

Harold Wiltshire's life in adult education spanned the apogee of the Labour movement paradigm, imaginative attempts to restructure it and its eventual demise. It seems appropriate, in a collection of essays dedicated to his memory, to review this process and look to the future. This is particularly fitting as his sparse writings touch on issues intensely relevant to the recomposition of adult education and the decentring of the working class and alternative social visions. This paper briefly examines the attempt to refurbish the links between university and labour and recharge the liberal tradition in the 1950s and 1960s as seen from Nottingham, the ascendancy and decline of the alternative pedagogy of industrial relations training and the prospects for a future in which calls of closing time are increasingly audible.

When the world was steady: revitalising the Great Tradition

... its interest lies not in learning for learning's sake but in learning as a means of understanding the great issues of life.

Harold Wiltshire (1956)

For Harold Wiltshire, 'trade union education' most obviously referred to the technical training unions gave their members in organisation and collective bargaining. What was important to him was workers' education, its distinctive curriculum the social studies, 'its typical student the reflective citizen' (Wiltshire, 1956: 89). Like his contemporaries he worried in the post-war years at the growing domination of traditional classes by the already educated. Consequently he sought to refashion workers' education through a focus on day release courses — often in the workplace — as an alternative to the evening classes which had characterised the progress of the inter-war years. The cachet and resources of an expanding university system and the collaboration of unions and management were deployed in a project which largely bypassed voluntarism although it involved the WEA as a junior partner. The development of the two-year and three-year day release courses in the coal industry from the early 1950s is well known (Mee, 1984). But from the late 1950s a network of day release courses was created covering a range of industries and employers in the Nottingham area, and further afield in Derby and Leicester, which came to comprise a substantial and impressive part of the Department's work (Thornton and Bayliss, 1965; Bayliss, 1991).

Wiltshire and his colleagues practised positive discrimination in relation to both students and pedagogy. His concern was to go beyond the educated minority to revitalise the liberal approach in face of the advance of technicism and vocationalism and the consequent blurring of important philosophical and pedagogic distinctions. To those in the university world who labelled attempts to distinguish between liberal education and technical training, as 'outmoded' he replied

> This is part of the cant of our time: understandable and well meaning cant, for it springs from a desire to rescue technical and vocational studies from the stupid disdain with which they have been regarded, but cant none the less. To assert that two things are equal is not to prove them identical ... to refuse to recognise obvious difference can lead neither to clear thinking or to sensible planning.
>
> Wiltshire (1956: 95)

Nottingham's conception of workers' education explicitly measured itself against the growth of technicism in trade union education. It sought whilst maintaining negotiation over the syllabus to provide students with a broad understanding of society:

> The basic subjects of the course, economics, industrial relations and communication were chosen because they comprise a study of contemporary industrial society. Issues which have specifically to do with employment do not dominate the course. It is not a training course for shop stewards.
>
> Thornton and Bayliss (1965: 24-5)

One potential problem for those who espoused older traditions linking learning and labour was the undifferentiated emphasis on *the worker* rather than *the worker as trade unionist* — and for those who supported a narrower instrumentalism — *the worker as shop steward*. It might be argued that early courses inadequately approached the practice of trade unionism. For both trainers and radicals Wiltshire probably emphasised the reflective citizen too much, the active citizen too little. If divorced to too great an extent from the problems of employment the study of economics or politics might appear too abstract although it must be insisted, this is a problem of successful pedagogic adaptation, of how the teaching and learning is structured and related to contemporary issues, not a problem of the *'relevance'* of economics or politics to workers. The answer then is to address how the social sciences should be properly taught and devise effective learning methods, not to remove them from the curriculum. Just as the solution to the real differences between education and skills training is not to blur distinctions, pretend one is the other, use 'liberal' as an evasive charm word but, rather to fuse them together, a process which developed to a greater extent at Nottingham in the 1960s and 1970s.

The Nottingham approach mirrored the strengths and weaknesses of the liberal tradition. In complete contrast to role training it asserted a broad, open, dynamic education. But it was underpinned by an ideology which mobilised the traditional liberating, but also the individualistic, integrative, civilising aspects of educational liberalism. Echoing the Oxford Report the creators of the courses in the coal industry argued

> it might be possible to build up over the years a sizeable body of men with some training in the collection and assessment of facts, in the dispassionate study of controversial problems. Such men ... might well provide a steadying, constructive and thoughtful element in local leadership. They might too find for themselves personal confidence and satisfaction in this opportunity to enlarge their knowledge.
>
> Thornton (1956: 198)

This benign, integrative, partisan vision mingled far from disruptively with that of National Coal Board managers who hoped the courses would create understanding of the need for cooperation in the newly nationalised industry and develop human capital and it melded with the conceptions of local union leaders who believed free intellectual inquiry would ultimately strengthen collectivism (Croucher and Halstead, 1990: 6-9). Conflict and class-based conceptions of industrial relations were never stressed — at least formally in descriptions of the courses and reports on them. Analysis of the work is studded with references to 'the social structure of the factory community', 'the problems of the factory community', the worker as citizen of 'an industrial society' (Thornton and Bayliss, 1965: 7-8). The flavour was sometimes that of Human Relations sociology: 'every social grouping including the grouping in industrial communities carries responsibilities towards the human beings it brings together'. The development of intellectual skills amongst its members, consequent on day release courses, would create a more efficient, cohesive community and 'clear if indirect benefit could accrue to employers'. Management, it was argued, welcomed courses because it is not effective opponents which management fears but blindly prejudiced, ignorant and inflexible attitudes and it is the process of liberating men from those which is the essential business of liberal study.

Thornton and Bayliss (1965: 19-20)

Consonant with the weaknesses of liberalism there is, here, the potential for illiberalism. It is sometimes easy to label the views of others 'prejudiced' or 'inflexible' when they are simply different. Liberating workers from 'ignorance' or 'inflexible attitudes' may entail genuine intellectual development. Or it may entail, in paternalistic practice, an attempt to replace ideas antagonistic to the success of the business enterprise with ideas functional to its economic logic. Civilising people may mean transforming their ideology and culture in our own interests. The contentious nature of these judgements — many managers do fear effective opponents, many problems in industry are not susceptible to 'rational' resolution — propelled a neutrality which downplayed the deep fissures in 'the industrial community' and decentred the central conflict over the price of labour and its utilisation which renders many problems insusceptible to solution simply through greater understanding and dispassionate reasoning.

This harmonious, organic, 'serving the industrial community' ideology in which community replaced class stemmed, perhaps, from a benign view of the success of post 1945 reformism and the ethos of an age in which capitalism appeared to have solved its major problems. It contrasts with formulations of workers' education which, recognising the continuing reality of class conflict, base themselves firmly on the working class and its institutions. But it reflected the power situation in which management controlled day release, the TUC increasingly wished to control the content of courses it supported — and there was no easy way forward. It chimed with the extra-mural departments' definition of their post 1945 mission: to serve *all* sections of the community. And it justified courses for a range of managerial and administrative groups placating those in the universities who viewed the education of trade unionists as partisan and demanded 'balance'. In the context of the limited resources available to extra-mural departments this approach undercut positive discrimination in favour of those educationally disadvantaged and interacted with other factors to limit the impact of work with trade unionists in redressing educational inequality (McIlroy, 1986).

The courses themselves reflected a diversity of approach personified, to take one example, in the very different figures of Fred Bayliss who broadly subscribed to the reformism of industrial relations orthodoxy in the 1950s and 1960s and worked for the National Board of Prices and Incomes, the Commission of Industrial Relations and the Department of Employment and Ken Coates, with Tony Topham the driving force of the Institute of Workers Control. Both were highly respected by students and colleagues as rigorous imaginative educators. And the very different work both conducted — together with many of their colleagues — outside the classroom makes nonsense of the claims of some that university workers' education was divorced from the practice of workers and failed to inform it. The 1960s was a decade of substantial advance. By the early 1970s the Department had eight full-time staff tutors involved in industrial studies. With the aid of WEA tutors and internal staff a strong corps of more than a dozen academics specialising in industrial relations, economics, sociology, psychology, labour history and labour law was deployed (University of Nottingham, 1971-2). Apart from the prolific output of Ken Coates on numerous aspects of trade unionism and politics other notable publications came from the department (see for example Bayliss, 1962; Goodman and Whittingham, 1969, 1973). Its research orientation was reflected in the establishment of *The Industrial Relations Journal* based for many years in the department with Brian Towers as its founding editor. The courses left a lasting impact on students and strengthened their role as union activists and officers, councillors and MPs (Mee, 1984: 23-32).

Nottingham in the heyday of industrial studies day release could not be taken as typical of university adult education for the work of departments differed, sometimes quite radically. Hull, Sheffield and Swansea appear to have taken more of an explicit trade union approach to a broad educational curriculum. Other departments such as Oxford embraced shop steward training to a greater degree.

Still others, such as Liverpool and Manchester, turned their hand to any industrial work which came along and of course many universities were only slightly involved (McIlroy, 1990a). This is why to counterpose the inefficient 'liberalism' of the extra-mural departments to the 'relevance' and vitality of the education developed by the unions themselves is to invoke a straw person. The work of some departments was very much in the training mould, its liberal appellation a worn if useful epithet which facilitated the flow of funding. The work of others, with industrial relations politicised and increasingly subject to state intervention, was, in its fusion of social education and practical skills arguably far more 'relevant' than TUC courses. The work of the best university educators grew out of the liberal tradition, reflecting its rigour, open debate, address of varied alternatives — but was far from confined by it. Their critical commitment to trade unionism allied to determination to explore all its dimensions, in the belief that theory should strengthen practice meant these courses represented a renewal of the radical social purpose tradition of workers' education associated with G.D.H. Cole.

A problem undoubtedly was the limits both DES and universities set on expansion and the resource demands of quality adult education. Harold Wiltshire noted this in the 1950s and by the end of the following decade one of his colleagues was pointing out 'perhaps the main restriction will be imposed by the universities themselves. Many of them still do not accept any responsibility for workers' education. They simply do not see it as their job' (Lawson, 1970: 13; Wiltshire, 1956: 96).

At their height in the 1960s the Nottingham courses were attended by only around 200 students (Bayliss, 1991: 17). Moreover, the TUC and the technical colleges were now in the field and Kenneth Lawson referred to 'a fear on the part of many tutors ... that the pressures for a more vocationally based type of course which comes from the trade unions and employers might be less easily resisted if there is too much competition' (1970: 13). The department's Deputy Director, Alan Thornton, noted that the TUC's priorities were 'rather limiting in scope' but felt the TUC scheme was 'likely to be widened to include the social and political objectives of the unions', observing optimistically

> the relationship on the ground between individual universities and their worker students and between particular universities and individual unions is now one of warmth, confidence and co-operation. It remains to establish the same kind of relationship between the universities and the TUC.
>
> Hughes and Thornton (1973: 157)

The failure of universities and unions to forge an alliance which could have developed the best of the long day release courses as part of a broad constellation of provision is one of the lost opportunities of workers' education. Weaknesses on either side might have been remedied and the legislation of 1975 have encompassed wider education as well as technical training. Perhaps, however, we are being unduly optimistic.

For what were involved were important differences of philosophy and a struggle for what the Labour movement should be about and who should define it. Collaboration was not to be. Instead a narrow definition of unions' institutional needs and hence trade unionists' educational requirements, mingled with historical antipathy to intellectuals and academics, was to win the day.

A disaffection: reinventing the shop steward

> He should think about why it is important they should learn some things rather than others, why he should want to change them in ways which he determines ...
>
> Harold Wiltshire (1973)

Harold Wiltshire and his colleagues at Nottingham believed, from a variety of different perspectives, that workers needed to understand the economic and political organisation of society if they were to make *their own* judgements about it and act upon them in their workplaces and industries and wider. In this sense curriculum flowed from student 'needs' perceived by programme planners as well as negotiation in the classroom. But as Wiltshire rightfully observed in his critique of liberal adult education, value-based assessment, selection and exclusion still operated.

> We do not simply perceive needs; in part we create them by a process of prescription or ascription ... [a course planner] should think about the criteria and value judgements that determine his ascription of need, his conception of what 'ought' to be in the programme.
>
> Wiltshire (1973: 29); and see Lawson (1973)

The conceptions of the TUC whose growing role attracted comment from Lawson and Thornton were very different to those informing the work of the Nottingham department. The TUC scheme established through its 1964 takeover of the NCLC and WETUC rejected in practice the emancipatory social purpose tradition on which these bodies based their work. Its commitment was to pluralism — conflict in industry was a reality but amenable to resolution by responsible unions and management committed to compromise generated via efficient procedures — and a growing impulse to corporatism, with the unions regulating their membership as part of a tripartite ordering of economy and society. The emphasis was therefore on organisational training to fashion unions as fit partners for employers and state. As fostered by union leaders such as Citrine and Bevin and later George Woodcock the object of union education was the union representative not the worker or Labour movement activist. Its mode was instruction, its mission socialisation, its curriculum inclusive of the mechanics of organisation and collective bargaining, exclusive of the knowledge and skills required to understand, reform or replace capitalism.

What was it for? Essentially the reproduction of the internal social relations of trade unionism committing what were after all *voluntary* officers to organisational culture and policy and their place in the hierarchy. And the efficient reproduction of external relations by inculcating the technical skills and knowledge required for formal relationships with employers and the state. Its purpose was to train stewards to behave properly. Without glossing over the deficiencies of the universities this was ideally, controlled, closed circuit training firmly asserted by the unions to be their own province. This latter claim, however, was handicapped by their lack of financial and educational resources which led in practice to a tense dependence on the educational bodies.

The infant pre-war trade union education was a somewhat sickly reflection of attempts to consolidate Labourism, marginalise leftism and workers control, strengthen the division between industrial and political in the Labour movement and concentrate relations between the two wings in the hands of a professional union hierarchy. It was of a limited nature and limited impact. In the post-war period the 'need' to integrate and professionalise lay officials, centralise authority in the unions and enhance the reach of the TUC intensified. As the post-war consensus crumbled, successive attempts at economic regeneration were perceived as foundering on the rocks of strong independent workplace organisation and inflationary workplace bargaining. The consensus was that unions needed to regain control of shop stewards and management of industrial relations if the state was to regain control of economic planning. A qualitative extension of shop steward training was recommended as part of this project (Royal Commission, 1968: 190-191; McIlroy, 1985).

The wage drift, unconstitutional stoppages, restrictive practices, viewed as a problem by the TUC, employers and state, were not viewed as a problem, certainly not in the same way, by many of the objects of concern, the shop stewards. As far as they were concerned they benefited from wage drift and restrictive practices and in many cases they had never had it so good (Goldthorpe, 1977). Their needs for training were diagnosed and prescribed for by doctors with a very different view of pathology. The TUC constructed the shop steward not as a potential activist at higher levels of the union, still less as an activist across the movement, participating in politics as the natural extension of economics. The shop steward as the subject of union education was composed as a workplace bargainer. But not as an aggressive militant: as a responsible union policy-loyal exponent of the industrial legality the TUC was so eager to reconstruct. From this flowed needs. From these ascribed needs flowed a curriculum based strongly on proceduralised collective bargaining.

The dominant purpose of TUC training, treated as crudely unproblematic by some writers, was to produce a *specific* trade unionism and a *particular species* of shop steward, developing through exhortation and training certain real tendencies, deflating others, to create a 'custodian of collective agreements, keeper of social order and realistic bargainer' (Lover, 1976: 29). To overcome recalcitrance to policy and realign workplace organisation with the needs of tripartism a curriculum was ordered

> which excludes consideration of [shop stewards'] wider educational needs as citizens or even potential general secretaries or cabinet ministers.
>
> > TUC (1968: 9)

Programme planners were urged in an elitist fashion which *a priori* excluded potential needs and the voices of stewards

> unions and other bodies before planning training courses need to assess thoroughly the needs of the workplace representative otherwise too much of the syllabus tends to be devoted to extensive general information on economics and industrial relations, to the neglect of subjects specifically related to the duties in which the representative is actively engaged.
>
> > TUC (1968: 21)

Wiltshire's insights on the value judgements informing needs ascription and their relevance for the problematic inclusive-exclusive process of role construction and curriculum creation could scarcely be better illustrated. The position that the major deficit in workplace trade unionism lay in formal organisational and bargaining skills is extraordinary. Unless, that is, we relate this judgement to the political context and the conflictual internal relations of trade unionism in this period. The 'problem' was the absence of *certain* skills or more precisely *certain attitudes* such as the ability to compromise, the ability to appreciate the desirability of incomes policy. And it was more obviously a problem for union leaders than for many of the stewards in whom they noted this deficiency. Partisan, artificial criteria of *relevance* and *priority* are being deployed. For it is far from clear, except in static, hierarchical, *power* terms why the general secretary needs a knowledge of economics whilst workplace representatives, faced daily with the consequences of economics, trapped or liberated by its implications, do not. The paternalism of TUC statements and of their defenders recalls Hirst's dictum 'saying what children need is only a cloaked way of saying what we judge they ought to have' (1974: 7). It is a commonplace that training downplaying examination of context, purpose and policy in trade unions or any organisation may lead to the status quo being taken for granted and further empower the powerful. The restriction of the curriculum to technical training may be seen as protecting 'the organisation' or 'the movement' against disaffection and the human power holders who hide behind this reification from alternative policies and disruptive political ideas (Fieldhouse, 1978: 39). The question is clearly posed as to whose 'needs' are best served by this approach: those of union leaders and their civil servants or those of activists and members?.

The TUC education specialists increasingly insisted that *their* conceptions of trade unionism and *their* conceptions of needs, reflecting TUC policy and, hence, their conceptions of a curriculum suitable for union representatives and their conceptions of learning methods must take precedence over those of teachers and students. It is neither conspiracy theory nor is it to impute base motives to union professionals to suggest that in constructing a political pedagogy in accord with state-union strategies and excluding critical interrogation of them, they are acting in their own interests and as 'servants of power' (c.f. Armstrong, 1982: 313). This process was of course facilitated by the centralised nature of the TUC scheme in which democracy was consciously limited as a matter of policy and in which the only formal decision-making body was the General Council (McIlroy, 1990b). Of course this is not to deny that this process of needs-meeting may not in itself create needs: the processes of labelling and supply can create acceptance and demand.

By the 1970s the TUC had created its own distinctive training antagonistic to open-ended, empowering, social education. It was disaffected and frustrated with the refusal of the universities in which it had lodged courses to fully and enthusiastically accommodate its goals. The long day release courses were rejected both in terms of their approach and the fact that more stewards could be trained if the length of courses was limited to ten days. They were not regarded as complementary to shorter provision but competitive with it, despite periodic rhetorical protestation that trade unionists needed both social education and skills training. There appeared little prospect of realising the sentiments of Nottingham and other universities that

> workers' education must be planned as an equal partnership between the trade unions and their educational partners, be they universities community or technical colleges.
>
> Hughes and Thornton (1973: 160)

Principled university educators had little alternative but to stand their ground. They could not confuse their purpose with that of the TUC apparatus or accept for one minute the definition of trade union education proffered by that apparatus.

> Both syllabus determination and student selection are as important to the tutors and the students as they are to the trade unions ... Training shop stewards to serve their members and training them to serve an existing union hierarchy are not necessarily the same thing ... If the fate of industry is too important to be left to the managers can we afford to leave the fate of trade union education exclusively in the hands of trade union officials?
>
> Park (1969: 99-100)

But were not those who believed in a critical education also, as Wiltshire suggested, working with and sometimes imposing their own version of needs? It would be wrong to deny that this happened: such imposition was an important ingredient in the 'control' strand of the liberal tradition and exclusion *did* operate (Fieldhouse, 1983). But the best educators in this tradition focused on the direct negotiation of curriculum and method by tutor and class, mobilising students' own perceptions of their needs whilst recognising the disparity of educational capital between teacher and students and the responsibility of the teacher to guide. This was a central device of direct democracy denied in the TUC scheme (McIlroy, 1990b). Moreover, some recognised with Harold Wiltshire the value ridden nature of curriculum construction and if less clearly, its power-driven evolution. Centrally the difference — and this was what made working within a committed liberal approach not simply preferable for committed educators but for trade union students — lay in the instructional dynamic of TUC training, its increasingly programmed basis, its limited address of the desirability of its purpose and alternative models of purpose, its silence over competing conceptions of union action and policy, its focus on technical skills as against issues and context.

The best university approach, in contrast, urged an embrace of the technical aspects of working class organisation and issues of immediate practical importance but insisted on relating them to a wider framework of social understanding as the essential means to enrich action. The best of the social purpose approach addressed a *variety* of ideological perspectives. The technical training approach was committed to trade unionism as collective bargaining to the exclusion of other conceptions of trade unionism and issues other than collective bargaining. In a very important sense the former approach was formally, explicitly, *open*: on what a steward was, on what trade unionism was, on which policies were preferable. In comparison the training model was formally *closed*, a closure represented by its dedication to programmed learning from TUC materials. Discussion of broader issues when it occurred was boundary-breaking, dysfunctional to the training model. For social purpose education it was central and organic. It is not surprising therefore that the social purpose education was perceived as a threat by those who wished to close matters of organisation and policy on their own terms. Contrariwise, for the committed educator this was an important quarrel to be pursued, not a matter for a non-aggression pact: 'you are right from your side, I am right from mine'. This could consign working class students—for all the resistance which might take place in the classroom — to a system based on instruction not critical education.

Nevertheless the necessities of the quasi-corporatist Social Contract, as perceived by the designers of union education, moved matters in the former direction. Legal rights to paid release were predicated on the relevance of curriculum to a shop steward's *industrial relations functions at the workplace*. In legislation and an ancillary Code of Practice the state directly defined the needs of stewards on the basis of the earlier TUC ascription and in the event of dispute the industrial tribunals and courts determined whether these statutory needs were properly reflected in course curricula. The creation of a state curriculum and the incarnation of the TUC as a responsible body reinforced earlier trends: against workers' education and social purpose and in favour of industrial relations training and responsible bargaining.

Given the nature of the TUC scheme and its own base Nottingham mounted no TUC courses. By 1980 there was some retrenchment owing to the growth of TUC courses, the increase in the provision of individual unions and harder attitudes by management to release of students. But the Department was still mounting around six one-year courses for workers from a mix of industries three of the two-year courses for miners — these were to terminate in 1984 — a Certificate in Industrial Relations and a Diploma in Political, Economic and Social Studies which recruited strongly from trade unionists. Six members of staff were significantly involved (Campbell and McIlroy, 1986: 6).

Other departments such as Leeds, Liverpool, Hull and Manchester were, until the 1980s, able to relate TUC syllabuses to a wider framework or balance mainstream provision against specialist courses or blur distinctions. By the end of that decade TUC courses had been removed from all universities in England and Wales with the exception of Sussex (UCACE, 1992). The new home for industrial relations training was the further eduction sector in 'institutions which are more prepared both to engage in a mechanistic training role ... and to surrender academic autonomy to a syllabus over whose drafting and content they have no control' (Taylor, 1982: 8). Nonetheless despite the serious decline of trade unionism and trade union education from 1980, some universities remained in the field taking advantage of the burgeoning of the educational work of the individual unions since 1975.

Industrial relations training declined through the 1980s and 1990s. State finance and regulation acted to stiffen its limits and restrict the possibilities of change, indeed the TUC moved to limit the space that had existed (McIlroy, 1995b). This was surprising. For if the skills training format had ever had any justification the ideological, political and economic fronts Thatcherism opened up against the Labour movement surely demonstrated the deficit lay elsewhere. Even within the limitations of a conjunctural needs-meeting paradigm were not other needs now more obvious and urgent? As one distinguished adult educator argued:

> Union representatives facing plant closures and redundancies, the re-organisation of working methods to secure higher productivity and new government legislation are equipped with skills which assume stable employment and a central role for local collective bargaining. They are skilled at conducting meetings, taking minutes and writing reports and they can calculate redundancy payments in seconds. But they have little understanding of the broader issues and of alternative economic and political strategies. As a result the demand is growing — so far it appears to come mainly from the

academics engaged in trade union education — for a shift of emphasis towards the study of economic and political questions.
Jennings (1982: 10) and see McIlroy (1980); Topham (1981)

TUC education had got along without direct state finance before 1975, rejecting offers of direct state funding because it saw they could essentially produce state control (TUC, 1970). What the TUC prophesied came to pass. The dependence common in corporatist arrangements soon set in and little attempt was made to confront the problem of the lack of funds for education unions generated themselves. Dependence was soon reinforced by loss of membership and continuing reverses on the industrial and political fronts. The TUC refused to replicate its initial opposition to the government in the political and industrial spheres on the educational front, eschewing campaigning or even critique for backstairs manoeuvring. The growth of institutional needs in unions has been well observed (Hyman and Fryer, 1975). Habituation to government funding meant its maintenance was now central and there would be no significant changes which could antagonise the state even if these appeared to be required by the changing industrial and political situation. Institutional maintenance, and preservation of the status quo were paramount and necessitated acceptance of government policy.

As in other areas of union reform the government took a step by step approach to an issue they felt merited fine-tuning rather than urgent surgery: shop steward training was relatively unthreatening (Tebbit, 1989; Fowler, 1989). A series of measures stiffened TUC resolve to stay within the state rubric of funding and curriculum. In 1983 employers were given rights to vet certain courses, in 1989 the rights to paid release were revised and in 1992 the end of direct grant aid was announced. Probings over materials on economic awareness and privatisation made clear where the power lay. The attitudes which produced a stultified, supine response throughout the period were highlighted in 1991 when at government behest the TUC banned the use of materials on courses on the grounds they were 'too political', counselled against any protest on the grounds that it might endanger the grant and urged that in future greater care should be taken to avoid criticisms of government policy in course materials. The willingness of the TUC to allow dependence on the state to form policy was demonstrated when the 1991 reform of further education tied funding to courses in a vocational, qualification or access mode. With alacrity the TUC announced it would explore accrediting its courses for NVQs: this, they surprisingly proclaimed, would strengthen workplace organisation (McIlroy, 1993a).

The years of neo-conservatism were, as Harold Wiltshire observed from the vantage point of an active retirement, years of 'narrow focus training' in which 'employability' and 'profitability' became almost the only criteria of educational success (1983: 10). The TUC's embrace of this ethos, its maintenance of 'narrow focus training' its attempts to take refuge from the harsh realities of economics and politics in workplace bargaining represented an important historical defeat for trade union education.

How late it was, how late: framing the future

> They will have the technical skills but they will lack and have to improvise means of developing conviction, commitment and a sense of purpose; without these technical skills are of little use. They will need tools that will enable them to take part in a continuing process of critical analysis ...
>
> Harold Wiltshire (1973)

In considering the future our first stop must be the trade unions themselves. If the rate of membership decline we have witnessed since 1979 continues there will be no future. For quite early in the next century there will be no trade unionists left to educate! Overall membership and density (% of labour force) declined from 12 million in 1979 to 8.9 million in 1992 and from 55% in 1979 to 37% in 1992. And decline is continuing (see Table 1). Membership of TUC affiliates tumbled from more than 12 million in 1979 to little more than 7 million in 1993 with density declining to around 30% of the labour force. It must be noted that decline is nothing new, nor is recovery: in the great days of workers' education in the 1920s and 1930s overall union density declined to 23%. Then as now the unions provided a central arena for working class education although we cannot gloss over the importance of the continuing downward curve of membership.

Is this, as some have suggested part of a dissolution of class, a move from class to community, from Fordism to 'New Times' with a consequent downgrading of trade unionism and trade union education? It would again be a mistake to minimise the importance of change. We are seeing significant changes in the structure of industry, the composition

Table 1: Union Membership and Density Selected Years

Year	Union Membership	Labour Force	Union Density
1920	8,348	18,469	45.2
1933	4,392	19,422	22.6
1945	7,865	20,400	38.6
1955	9,751	21,913	44.5
1965	10,325	23,385	44.2
1975	12,026	23,587	51.0
1979	13,447	24,264	55.4
1985	10,821	21,418	41.1
1992	8,928	21,354	36.7

Source: McIlroy, 1995a

of the labour force and the economic context, with strong tendencies to globalisation of capital and internationalisation of trade. That we are witnessing significant restructuring is undeniable. To view these changes as 'a transition from one regime to accumulation to another within capitalism' (Hall, 1990: 126) is at least premature if we scrutinise rather than inflate the evidence available. Post Fordism and 'New Times' depend on a caricature of Fordism and their progenitors produce inadequate evidence to demonstrate that mass markets for standardised products are disintegrating, that flexible specialisation is becoming dominant or that the workforce is finally structured between a privileged 'core' and an exploited periphery (Hyman, 1991; Pollert, 1991). Recent events in the European Union demonstrate at one and the same time strong tendencies towards internationalisation *and* the continuing power of the individual state and national polity. Globalism still has clear limits and the nation state powerful purchase (Callinicos, 1989: 132-44).

What is occurring is not a *withering away* of class but a *remaking* of class — of course it is a remaking which affects cohesion and unity, culture and consciousness. But let us recall that half a century ago sociologists observed the 'ladder like stratification of the working class with many small rungs' (Zweig, 1948: 84). There are undoubtedly changes in ways of seeing, in sense of community and culture, in identification with the institutions of labourism. In sharp contrast with those adult educators who predicate a move from class to community deploying the work of Stuart Hall and *Marxism Today*, work which is seriously lacking in empirical ballast, authoritative analysis assures us that Britain remains a class society not a post class society (Goldthorpe and Marshall, 1992). Class remains as much the basis for material and ideological conflict today as it was thirty years ago (Evans, 1993). The ideological impact of the new right has, as numerous surveys over the last decade confirm, been limited, its political victories achieved with 42% of the vote (Butler and Kavanagh, 1992). The economic and industrial conditions, the unregulated capitalism that bred trade unionism remain whilst trade unions are significantly more popular (McIlroy, 1995a: 385-408). Despite its successes Thatcherism has failed to secure the extended popular consent that certain intellectuals, who tend to over-estimate ideology, credit it with. Rather, successive volumes of *Social Trends* depict an electorate which is often to the left of the Labour Party and which rejects key aspects of market ideology accepted as part of the new consensus by the political elite. Even Conservative supporters often yearn for a 'one nation Britain' (Gamble, 1994: 236-241; Whitely et al., 1994).

What does stand out is the *political* disorientation of the Labour movement, the decline of any strong sense of social mission, in part a response to the political offensive of the New Right and the defeat of the hopes of the 1960s and 1970s, in part attributable to an internal disarray more obvious in the new conditions — and all accelerated by the collapse of the regimes in the USSR and Eastern Europe and the apparent global triumph of a restructured more brutal capitalism. One manifestation has been the desertion of intellectuals pursuing what is now a historic journey not only from Marxism but from progressive, humanist socialist projects of transformation. This has been reflected in adult education in the dabbling with New Times and post-modernism and the irresponsible — intellectually and socially — retreat from class.

Pessimism *is* in order: a facile optimism evades the real problems. It is not helpful, for example, to simply characterise the failures of planning as the fruits of bureaucratic Stalinism or elitist social democracy when they also reflect real historic weaknesses in socialist thinking about economics, social organisation and human motivation. Nonetheless we need a sense of history, internationalism and perspective. The left has seen defeat before. The 'end of history' and 'the end of ideology' have been falsely proclaimed before by false prophets. The demise of Stalinism and the upheavals in Eastern Europe, the coming on stage of the newly industrialised countries provides new opportunities. We have to look not only at the problems in Britain but the challenge and the new weight lent to what must be international struggles by the emerging working class in Brazil, China, India, South Africa, Taiwan, Korea, Malaysia and many other countries. We have already remarked on the real limits of change particularly ideological change. The latest 'State of the Nation' survey follows its predecessors showing 46% agreeing with the statement 'More socialist planning would be the best way to solve Britain's economic problems' as against 28% disagreeing (*Guardian*, 1994). There are beliefs there to be developed and mobilised.

The Labour movement remains, if weakened, an organisational and aspirational reality. It possesses a breadth, a 'rootedness' and a potential power other progressive interest groups lack. It can still provide an anchorage and source of strength for educational movements. In the absence of any other potential agency for change the organisations of the working class remain an important arena in which adult education can engage with the urgent issues of the day and develop the dialectic between class and community, class and sexual and ethnic identity. For what are the alternatives? Adult educators have been pressurised by government policies and the new market to involve themselves in vocational training, usually for the better educated, or consumerism to facilitate self actualisation, personal growth and problem solving for the middle classes. Access work and community education provide routes more consonant with adult education's tradition of social engagement; they can relate to work with trade unionists rather than substitute for it. If we believe in the role of active human agency and pedagogic intervention in social change we will not see currently depressing trends as eternal or allow them to privilege escape and apathy. We will cultivate hope and keep alive the conception of adult education as a progressive social movement.

> If we are to work effectively we must, I think, assume that present restrictions will not last for ever and that they will be succeeded by periods of growth and development.
>
> Wiltshire (1983: 5)

The direction the education of trade unionists should take is clear. Trade unionism faces a wide range of threats and challenges deriving from contemporary social, economic and political change. The education of trade unionists should address those challenges and the range of possible response. Capitalism today seems at once more secure and more volatile. Markets are harder and there is increased competition between states to attract capital on capital's terms. Moves towards globalisation of capital and trade constrain economic management at the level of the individual state and internationalisation seems to circumscribe important areas of intervention witnessed in the EU's commitment to the ERM and Maastricht. This has an impact on traditional central goals of the Labour movement such as full employment and increased public expenditure which if implemented in their turn strengthen trade unions. The new consensus restricts state intervention in industry and supports privatisation and enterprise culture.

Changes in industrial structure and labour force composition are similarly unfavourable to trade unionism and intimately related to its decline in the brave new world where Sainsburys employs more workers than Ford and Equity has more members than the NUM. The move from manufacturing to services; large to small workplaces; public to private industry; full time to part time work; higher sustained levels of unemployment; the increased participation of women in the labour force; all these trends present multi-faceted challenges to union philosophy, organisation and culture. So of course do important changes in technology and management strategy centred on Human Resource Management and the urgent need to resurrect the issue of industrial democracy. Politically the unions are faced with an important restructuring of their traditional relationship with the Labour Party, and wider, the tribulations of their continuing engagement with the EU. Culturally and ideologically they have been faced with an assault not only from the New Right but from within Labourism, assaults trade union education has done precious little to answer.

The education of trade unionists should be far more about delineating and understanding these changes, far less about workplace industrial relations. It should be less about shop stewards and more 'about the working class as a topic of study, a range of experiences and as an agency for social change' (Fryer, 1990: 227). More about the Labour movement and its place in the world and all its concerns, less about collective bargaining. This is not to say trade union education should not be about the workplace or bargaining, simply that these issues are not in themselves a fitting basis for it but should have their place integrated in a wider curriculum and a wider vision. This emphasis will make the education of trade unionists less the marginal closed-off area it has been and more linked to community education, continuing education and the wider educational system. And if such education is to be more about the working class it has to address differences within the working class, the changing position of women workers, the reality of sexual and ethnic division and oppression, not pay lip service to them.

A broad economic, political and social education; an education which is international in its reach, critical in its approach, an education in which action flows from understanding; an education which rejects opportunistic, self interested criteria of *relevance and priority* which in the end are self-defeating; this will be a fitting education, one which will provide trade unionists with the maps, compasses and weapons to confront the new century. But it must be, above all, a *democratic* education. It cannot be forged through 'needs meeting' and imposition, only through genuine dialogue between teachers and students (McIlroy, 1995b).

When we turn to the current position in trade union education the challenge of realising such a vision seems breathtaking — at least for those of us who believed in the past in the possibility of a national well-resourced system of labour education with an important role for universities.

Table 2 TUC Day Release Courses — 1976-93 Selected Years

	Introductory Stage 1 & 2		Health and Safety Courses		Short Courses	
Year	Courses	Students	Courses	Students	Courses	Students
1976-7	752	10,917	578	7,803	-	-
1979-80	1,208	15,701	1,441	18,738	-	-
1982-3	896	11,724	526	6,737	-	-
1986-7	762	9,564	565	6,973	1,183	14,401
1990-1	613	6,794	581	6,741	1,340	15,529
1992	512	6,045	521	6,457	1,198	15,499

Source: TUC Reports

Table 2 demonstrates the sustained decline of TUC courses in recent years. To provide some perspective, the TUC in the late 1970s aimed at the annual provision of 190,000 training places on ten-day courses, half of these to be provided through its own programme. The massive shortfall has to be related to declining membership, although in the first half of the 1980s the numbers of workplace representatives increased and turnover amongst representatives. By 1986 only between 10% and 15% of representatives received *any* training and this might mean only of a day's duration (TUC, 1986, 1987). Decline is likely to accelerate given dependence on state funding: without immediate action by the General Council the infrastructure which delivers TUC regional courses would have collapsed in the first term of 1994 (TUC, 1993: 47). Affiliated unions are not willing to make up the shortfall and the TUC is not prepared to divert funds from other sources on a long term basis (TUC, 1994).

These courses are now almost completely a further education affair. In 1982-3, eleven of the old universities still mounted TUC courses although the total number of such courses was under 100. A decade later only one university was involved (Campbell and McIlroy, 1986; UCACE, 1992). Only a small number of the new universities seem to offer courses specifically for trade unionists although there are no statistics available.

The unions' own provision has constituted a complicated mosaic. It is worth noting again the incongruous situation where both the national union federation and its affiliates provide often overlapping skills training and the provision of wider education is often left to affiliates who might be thought best fitted and, in the case of the bigger unions most able, to train their own representatives in specific nuts and bolts. The unions have provided annually roughly the same amount of student places as the TUC, 28,000 compared with 23,000 from the TUC by the mid 1980s. UNISON, the biggest affiliate, has a particularly impressive programme at both national and district level with courses mounted in house and with universities and colleges. The TGWU too has sustained much of the progress of the 1970s. At the start of that decade it was spending around £50,000 annually on education but by the end of the 1980s that had increased tenfold (SIT/TGWU, 1988, 16). The General Municipal and Boilermakers' courses are largely residential and internally resourced and the same applies to the Electrical and Engineering Union on a lesser scale. With the smaller unions the tendency is to grater reliance on the TUC programme.

Work with unions such as UNISON and the TGWU has provided a source of sustenance to universities over the last decade. Nonetheless, as Table 3 demonstrates, the picture in the older universities is in quantitative terms unprepossessing.

Many of these courses give cause for encouragement. Some specifically originated in analysis of the inadequacies of the TUC scheme. The TGWU, for example, noted:

> In the present economic and political situation many trade union representatives have begun to see a need to study the broader economic and political issues and at the same time to keep the knowledge within the framework of the union and build it on to their shop steward training.
>
> Fisher (1984: 4)

Table 3: Universities and Trade Unions 1992, 1993

	Full time staff	Courses	Enrolments	FTEs
Bangor	2	9	113	13.5
Durham	1	6	83	12
Hull	2	53	614	46
Leeds	2	70	-	42
Manchester	1	12	230	33
Nottingham	2	10	120	-
Sheffield	3	7	112	24
Southampton	2	7	-	12
Surrey	6	223	3,296	173
Sussex	1	4	50	10

Source: UCACE, 1992, updated where possible to 1993. Almost all 'full-time' staff are now involved in other organising and teaching in contrast with the past.

On this basis year-long courses, partly in a distance learning mode, were developed with the Universities of Surrey, Leeds, Liverpool, Manchester and Northumbria. UNISON has developed similar work with Nottingham, Manchester and Sheffield. Surrey has created a major programme based on work with the TGWU with courses of every kind and description and a strong emphasis on developing lay tutors. This has been emulated in a smaller way at Hull where many of the older traditions of the longer day release courses are maintained and work based on collaborative research projects had been mounted with local trade union groups and local authorities. Leeds has been able to maintain three or four two-year courses recruiting generally from trade unionists, develop training courses for full-time officers with USDAW and a number of worker research projects based on MSF and the TGWU. Southampton has worked with the Royal College of Nursing and provided health and safety courses for a number of unions.

Overall this traditional work with unions is slender and perched precariously on the edge of university continuing education. It is maintained by an ageing workforce producing often personalised, customised provision together with a penumbra of part-time tutors. In many cases the exit of current staff would mean they were not replaced. This provision is therefore tenuous and likely to decline further, a view strengthened by current developments in university continuing educa-tion generally. The tendency to replace the academic extra-mural department with administrative units continues to gain momentum accompanied by changes in funding which encourage moves to accreditation. Neither of these developments is likely to help the programme in trade union studies which is 'messy' in administrative terms, requires intensive but unpredictable organisational input and still often recruits from students whose full-time education terminated at sixteen.

The pressures are clearly towards credentialling. In a sense this is the legacy of history. The TUC's drive to technicise shop steward training and in consequence locate it in the technical college sector laid the ground for its assimilation to the new vocationalism. The termination of the state grant strengthened the move towards NVQs stimulated by the 1992 legislation's mandate to the Further Education Funding Council to foster provision leading to NVQs. By the 1990s TUC education had lost any real independence and was locked into a relatively straightforward stimulus — response pattern to state initiatives. We have only to compare these two statements separated by a mere three years.

> TUC course aims do not set criteria that students meet to succeed against some objective standard. This is not possible and it is not desirable ...
>
> TUC (1990)

> ... both the aims and content of TUC courses as well as the main delivery infrastructure will benefit considerably from the development of standards for voluntary union officers. Training for union representatives is as essential as any vocational training in industry and should be similarly treated.
>
> TUC (1993: 47)

By 1994, the TUC was describing its education centre as 'an assessment centre' and advertising for staff to develop assessment procedures and 'the design and delivery of standards-based training programmes' (*New Statesman, 1994*). Yet the NVQ system it was so enthusiastic about has been subject to detailed critique on a very wide range of grounds and characterised as 'a disaster of epic proportions' (Smithers, 1994). The central idea of 'competence' trivialises the processes of human action, downplays the knowledge and critical thinking central to action and education and provides a crude and ineffective base for measurement (Ashworth and Saxton, 1990). Historically, trade union education eschewed even superior, more sophisticated forms of assessment on the grounds that attainment could only be assessed within a *collective* context and a specific economic and political framework (Miller and Stirling, 1991: 210). The introduction of NVQs makes explicit, extends and systematises the training basis of courses. It will individualise training, reinforce the already powerful emphasis on skills and introduce a partisan, divisive and inadequate conception of the *incompetent* shop steward who if we are addressing knowledge, principle, commitment and critical thinking may be extremely competent. It can strengthen individualism within the unions and the dangerous idea, already embodied in these courses, that representing the union involves mastery of a range of process skills and techniques — rather than strategic thinking and power building techniques — ultimately licensed by and measured by the state (McIlroy, 1993b). The NVQ system, applied to union education, can be a further means for the disciplining and surveillance of shop stewards and their commitment to certain goals and practices, to one kind of trade unionism, as against others.

> With competence there is closure, all learners are tied into a centrally determined predefined set of goals whose meaning and practice are circumscribed. The goal of learning is competence demonstrated in a specific set of ways, nothing more, nothing less.
>
> Edwards and Usher (1994: 12)

A majority of union officers are said to be opposed to the introduction of NVQs (Howard, 1994). And so are a majority of tutors who teach on these courses in further education colleges (NATFHE, 1993). Their views are brushed aside: by 1995 the TUC appeared to be determined to press ahead with the imposition of a system of accreditation by the Open College based on NVQ style 'occupational standards'. Scrutiny of the proposed system suggests it falls foursquare within the crude competency mode: it is thus likely to constrain genuine learning on courses (Hyland, 1993; and see Moore and Jones, 1993). The introduction of the system could buttress the TUC's flaking national role but it could also encounter opposition from powerful affiliates with strong education schemes of their own.

It will certainly cut most university tutors off from links with mainstream TUC provision and points us towards the alternative of access and credit provision. A number of the new universities have recently developed evening courses supported by the TUC which gives access to, or credit for, diploma or degree courses. Some of the former polytechnics notably the University of South Bank have developed certificate courses and BA degrees in the social sciences with Labour Studies Pathways whilst the University of Northumbria recruits trade unionists to a BA in Labour Studies. In the traditional sector MAs in Labour Studies are projected at Manchester and Warwick whilst we must not forget the imaginative way the residential colleges such as Ruskin, Coleg Harlech and Northern College, now linked with Hallam University, have overcome recent difficulties and plugged into the new system of higher education.

It would be a pity if the traditions of liberal education were to be lost but Table 3 tells its own tale. There will still in the immediate future be earmarked HEFC funding for liberal provision and work with the disadvantaged but with the prevailing winds blowing towards degree work, research and accreditation there is a big question mark over the long term future of such funding. Harold Wiltshire wanted passionately to maintain an education which involved students neither as technicians, functionaries nor as examinees. It looks very much as if in many cases the only way of maintaining an educational approach will mean compromising over assessment. The UNISON courses at Nottingham, Manchester and Sheffield have demonstrated that it is possible to maintain the essentials of the social purpose tradition within a credential mode. As credit transfer develops it will be possible to link in a wide range of provision whilst hopefully maintaining non credit courses at the same time.

This could represent a redefinition with the training of shop stewards finally becoming a vocational organisational matter and the wider trade union education becoming a more diffuse education of trade unionists. This would be a pity. For many trade unionists continue to demonstrate keen interest in real education. In the 1980s Roy Moore noted 'the great thirst' for making explicit the political and economic dimensions of trade unionism whenever he 'was able to loosen the reins on narrower instrumental teaching' (1981: 53). In recent years I have had many productive course introduction and course assessment sessions with TGWU and UNISON representatives who strongly support this position. We also encounter intriguing hints of the limits of needs meeting. In one TUC survey only 2% of respondents mentioned 'development of skills' as a keyword in assessing how useful courses are, 'disconcertingly low given the emphasis on skills throughout the course' (Mahon and Stirling, 1988: 55). It is difficult to resist Smith's conclusion about much of existing trade union education.

In failing to provide the student with a sense of perspective necessary to understand society in its concrete, inter-related totality these
courses have been unsuccessful in safeguarding the traditions of
workers education. The TUC courses attempt to assist trade unionists to tackle their immediate employment problems and little else.
By being so narrowly conceived the courses do not provide for the
broader educational needs of workers.

Smith (1984: 87)

As we have argued, the extent to which one can successfully tackle
'immediate employment problems' without going beyond these symp-
toms to their roots is highly questionable; distinctions between 'educational needs' and 'trade union needs' are dubious ones. To be educated
as a trade unionist is to be educated in economics and politics and
history and sociology. The drive to 'prioritise' 'relevant' skills training,
ideologically constructed by professionals, fragments an essential educational unity between education to develop a critical understanding of
the economic, political and ideological forces that influence trade
unionism and the skills for action that flow from it. Within this unity
skills are important but secondary. We can draw no rigorous relationship between the hegemony of workplace skills training from 1975 and
the decline of British trade unionism. But it is clear that even within the
confines of Labourism and the tenuous rubric of 'relevance and priority'
the case for an education in which union representatives can critically
analyse the organisation and politics of the Labour movement remains,
particularly in the light of recent disasters, an urgently compelling one.
In its pervasive emphasis on technical skills and the workplace and its
amputation of critical issue-based education, steward training has
reflected the weaknesses of trade unionism, not sought to transcend
them. The future challenge is to reintegrate skills training and wider
education in the best traditions of the long day release courses which
Harold Wiltshire supported long ago in Nottingham. We can never go
back, never simply emulate the past. We still have a lot to learn from it.

References

Armstrong, P. (1982). The needs-meeting ideology in liberal adult education. *International Journal of Life long Education*, 1, 4.

Ashworth, P. and Saxton, J. (1990). On competence. *Journal of Further and
Higher Education*, XIV, 2.

Bayliss, F. (1962). *British Wages Councils*. Blackwell.

Bayliss, F. (1991). Day release courses at Nottingham. *The Industrial Tutor*, 5,4.

Butler, D. and Kavanagh, D. (1992). *The British General Election of 1992*. Macmillan.

Callinicos, A. (1989). *Against Post-Modernism*. Polity Press.

Campbell, A. and McIlroy, J. (1986). Trade union studies in British Universities: changing patterns, changing problems. *International Journal of Lifelong Education*, 5, 3.

Croucher, R. and Halstead, J. (1990). The origin of liberal adult education for miners at Sheffield. *Trade Union Studies Journal*, 21.

Edwards, R. and Usher, R. (1994). Disciplining the subject: the power of competence. *Studies in the Education of Adults*, 26.1.

Evans, G. (1993). The decline of class divisions in Britain? *British Journal of Sociology*, 44, 3.

Fieldhouse, R. (1978). *The Workers Educational Association: Aims and Achievements 1903-77*. University of Syracuse.

Fieldhouse, R. (1983). The ideology of English adult education teaching 1925-50. *Studies in the Education of Adults*, 15, 2.

Fisher, J. (1984). *Report to the TGWU on the 1983-4 Distance Learning Course*. University of Surrey.

Fowler, N. (1989). Correspondence with the author.

Fryer, B. (1990). The challenge to working class education. In *The Search for Enlightenment* (ed. B. Simon). Lawrence and Wishart.

Gamble, A., (1994). *The Free Economy and the Strong State: the politics of Thatcherism*, 2nd edition. Macmillan.

Goldthorpe, J. (1977). Industrial relations in Great Britain: a critique of reformism. In *Trade Unions Under Capitalism* (eds. T. Clarke and L. Clements). Fontana.

Goldthorpe, J. and Marshall, G. (1992). The promising future of class analysis. *Sociology*, 26, 3.

Goodman, J. and Whittingham, T. (1969). *Shop Stewards in British Industry*. McGraw Hill.

Goodman, J. and Whittingham, T. (1973). *Shop Stewards*. Pan Books.

The Guardian (1994). 'State of the Nation', 21 September.

Hall, S. (1990). The meaning of New Times. In *New Times* (S. Hall and M. Jacques). Lawrence and Wishart.

Hirst, P. (1974). *Knowledge and the Curriculum*. Routledge.

Howard, S. (1994). 'No verifiable quality', *Morning Star*, 26 August.

Hughes, H.D. and Thornton, A. (1973). The British experience and present situation. In *The Role of Universities in Workers' Education*. ILO, Geneva.

Hyland, T. (1993). Mismatches, paradoxes and square circles: Making NVQs fit adult learning. *Adults Learning*, 4, 10.

Hyman, R. (1991). Plus ca change: the theory of production and the production of theory. In *Farewell to Flexibility* (ed. A. Pollert). Blackwell.

Hyman, R. and Fryer, R. (1975). Trade unions: sociology and political economy. In *Processing People* (ed. J. McKinlay). Holt, Rinehard and Winston.

Jennings, B. (1982). *Trade Union Education in Britain*. European Centre for Leisure and Education.

Lawson, K. (1970). Workers' education in Britain. *International Labour Review*, 10, January-June.

Lawson, K. (1973). The justification of objectives in adult education. *Studies in Adult Education*, 5, 1.

Lover, J. (1976). Shop steward training — conflicting objectives and needs. *Industrial Relations Journal*, 7, 1.

Mahon, P. and Stirling, J. (1988). 'I can do that': the impact of trade union education. *The Industrial Tutor*, 4,7.

McIlroy, J. (1980). Politics and the trade unions: why the issue is one the Labour movement must take up. *Tribune*, 10 October.

McIlroy, J. (1985). Adult education and the role of the client — the TUC education scheme 1929-1980. *Studies in the Education of Adults*, 13,2.

McIlroy, J. (1986). Review of G. Mee 1984. *Bulletin of the Society for the Study of Labour History*, 51, 1.

McIlroy, J. (1990a). The triumph of technical training. In *The Search for Enlightenment* (ed. B. Simon). Lawrence and Wishart.

McIlroy, J. (1990b). 'If rightly understood ....' Union education and the question of democracy. *International Journal of University Adult Education*, XXXIX, 3.

McIlroy, J. (1993a). Tales from smoke-filled rooms. *Studies in the Education of Adults*, 25, 1.

McIlroy, J. (1993b). What's happening to trade union education. *Trade Union News*, November.

McIlroy, J. (1995a). *Trade Unions in Britain Today*. 2nd edition. Manchester University Press.

McIlroy, J. (1995b), The dying of the light? A radical look at trade union education. In *Adult Education, Critical Intelligence and Social Change* (eds. M. Mayo and J. Thompson). NIACE.

Mee, G. (1984). *Miners, Adult Education and Community Service 1920-1984*, University of Nottingham, Department of Adult Education.

Miller, D. and Stirling, J. (1991). Evaluating trade union education. In *Research as Engagement* (eds. K. Forrester and C. Thorne). University of Leeds, Department of Adult Education.

Moore, R. (1981). Political Education in Practice. *Industrial Tutor*, 3,5.

Moore, R. and Jones, L. (1993). Education, competence and the control of expertise. *British Journal of the Sociology of Education*, 14, 4.

NATFHE (1993). Assessment on trade union courses.

New Statesman (1994), 20 May.

Park, T. (1969). Trade union education. In *Trade Union Register* (eds. K. Coates, T. Topham and M. Barratt Brown). Spokesman.

Pollert, A. (ed.) (1991). *Farewell to Flexibility*. Blackwell.

Royal Commission on Trade Unions and Employers Associations (1968). *Report*. HMSO.

Smith, T. (1984). Trade union education — its past and future. *Industrial Relations Journal*, 15, 2.

Smithers, A. (1994). Quoted in *Financial Times*, 18 August.

Society of Industrial Tutors and Transport and General Workers' Union, (1988). *The Impossible Dream: The Future of Paid Educational Leave in Britain*.

Taylor, R. (1982). *Recent Developments in University Adult Education: A Socialist Critique*. University of Leeds, Department of Adult Education.

Tebbit, N. (1989). Correspondence with author.

Thornton, A. (1956). Day release for liberal studies. *Adult Education*, 29, 3.

Thornton, A., and Bayliss, F. (1965). *Adult Education and the Industrial Community*. National Institute of Adult Education.

Topham, T. (1981). The need for political education. *The Industrial Tutor*, 3, 5.

TUC (1968). *Training Shop Stewards.*

TUC (1970). *Supplementary Evidence to Russell Committee on Adult Education.*

TUC (1986). *Trade Unions and the Economy: Notes for Tutors.*

TUC (1987). *Review of the TUC Education Service.*

TUC (1990). *Aims and Methods in Trade Union Education.*

TUC (1993). *Report.*

TUC (1994). Trade Union Education Review Group, *TUC Education Service Funding.*

UCACE (1992). *Trade Union Work in Departments.*

University of Nottingham, Department of Adult Education (1971-2). *Annual Report.*

Whitely, P., Seyd, P. and Richardson, J. (1994). *True Blues, The Politics of Conservative Party Membership*. Oxford University Press.

Wiltshire, H. (1956). The great tradition in university adult education. *Adult Education*, XXIX, 2. Reprinted in *The Spirit and the Form* (ed. A. Rogers, 1976). Department of Adult Education, University of Nottingham.

Wiltshire, H. (1973). The concepts of learning and need in adult education. *Studies in Adult Education*, 5,1.

Wiltshire, H. (1983). The role of the university adult education department. *Studies in the Education of Adults*, 15, 2.

Zweig, F. (1948). *Labour, Life and Poverty*. Gollancz.

Distance Education and The Great Tradition

Desmond Keegan

Context

If one attempted to analyse educational provision from the point of view of distance education one might identify three differing structures: conventional provision; teaching at a distance; teaching face-to-face at a distance. Each of these complements the others and enriches the possibilities of offering education to learners.

Conventional education

Conventional provision is the normal offering of education in schools, colleges and universities today. Most histories of Western education, like Boyd and King's *The History of Western Education* (1969), trace it back to Plato and the Greeks some 2500 years ago. Its characteristic structures are the dialogue, the lecture developed by the medieval universities, the tutorial and seminar added by the humanists and, more recently, the laboratory practical, the field trip and the periods of study in the library or resource centre.

Unesco statistics tell us that there are about 600,000,000 students, mainly children, in our education systems today and, very broadly, one might suggest that their education was characterised by (i) face-to-face contact (ii) between teacher and learner in the learning group (iii) with interpersonal communication.

Distance education

The history of teaching at a distance begins 150 years ago. Distance education was not possible without the developments of technology, especially in transportation and communication, associated with the Industrial Revolution.

Teaching at a distance is characterised by the separation of teacher and learner and of the learner from the learning group, with the interpersonal face-to-face communication of conventional education being replaced by an apersonal mode of communication mediated by technology. As a result the first 100 years of distance provision were clouded by criticism and hesitancy. This form of education is provided today by correspondence schools, open universities and distance or external departments of conventional colleges and universities. The development of open universities in the 1970s brought rapid improvements in the quality and quantity of provision and led to heightened status. By 1995 more than 20,000,000 students, most of them adults, were studying at a distance worldwide.

For the last 150 years educational provision has been enhanced by the availability of courses at a distance. This has provided a useful complement to conventional schools, colleges and universities, especially for those unable or unwilling to attend them.

Teaching face-to-face at a distance

The possibility of teaching face-to-face at a distance was achieved by an electronics revolution in the 1980s. The deregulation of the telecommunications industry allied to the speeding up of chips and the introduction of broadband technologies brought about this veritable revolution. The German scholar, O. Peters (1994), had argued that there was something unsettling about a form of education (distance education) in which interpersonal communication and face-to-face interaction in the learning group were eliminated, as these were regarded as cultural imperatives for education in East and West. Now these characteristics can be electronically recreated.

Virtual or electronic classrooms can now be linked by satellite or by compressed video codec technology or by full bandwidth links, making it possible for the first time in history to teach face-to-face at a distance. The lecturer can see and hear the students present in the class and also all the other students at the other sites hundreds or thousands of kilometres away. All the students at all the locations can see and hear the lecturer and all other students in the system. The interaction of face-to-face education has been recreated electronically.

As the 21st century approaches, conventional face-to-face teaching in schools, colleges and universities continues to prosper but it is complemented by correspondence, audio, video and computer technologies from correspondence schools and open universities throughout the world. Both are enriched by the availability of virtual systems in which the face-to-face interpersonal communication of conventional education can be achieved at a distance.

The Great Tradition

In *The Spirit and the Form*, Wiltshire (1956; 1976) delineated five characteristics of the Great Tradition which give a challenging framework for the interpretation of distance education systems as they have evolved over the last 150 years.

Commitment to a humane curriculum

Since their inception distance education and distance training have been pragmatic in their curriculum. The ideal has invariably been to provide the most economic way of getting from enrolment to examination for students who are unable to attend college and who frequently have employment, family and social responsibilities in addition to their study programme.

Concern for the social sciences

Wiltshire's concern for the social and the humane is not shared by distance education and training. The field has had, it is true, its humanists like Wedemeyer from Wisconsin in the United States and Holmberg from Malmö in Sweden but, in the main, the 'great issues of life' have not been the focus of distance education.

A non-vocational attitude

The vast majority of distance education courses at universities are certification-focused, leading directly to examinations and awards at certificate, diploma and degree level. In the same way the staple distance training courses both from government institutions (France, Australia, New Zealand) or from proprietary ones, has been accountancy, mathematics, adult second chance and other vocationally-oriented subjects.

Equality of educational opportunity

The democratisation of educational provision has been a dimension of distance education since its beginnings. It emancipated learners from the timetabling of lectures and from the requirement of joining a learning group in order to learn. In systems where longitudinal research studies have been carried out over decades, the University of New England at Armidale for instance (Smith, 1979), it has been demonstrated with a fair amount of conclusiveness that adults studying at a distance (say on a farm in New South Wales) can score just as well as recent high school graduates, and sometimes win the prize for the best student on the course or the best student at the university. This applies even for mature age students who had failed to reach matriculation at school or who had failed matriculation, in courses in which both groups of students are studying the same curriculum, submitting the same assignments to the same tutors, and sitting the same university examinations.

The Socratic method in small tutorial groups

Printed learning materials quickly established themselves as the favoured didactic strategy of distance education. Frequently these were developed under the influence of behaviourist psychological ideas and later adopted ideas from systems analysis. This militated against the Socratic approach and tutorial interchange because the course developers set strict learning objectives and chose one of many possible solutions or approaches for presentation, thereby blocking the students from other paths.

Central concepts

The idea of a university

Distance training courses (vocational and further education courses at lower than university level) have been accepted for decades as a valid form of vocational qualification and it has recently been claimed (Devlin, 1993) that they now form a preferred option for some international and multinational corporations. It was only in the 1990s, however, that the validity of university degrees, won partially or wholly at a distance, was grudgingly conceded by the academic community. A major factor in this gradual acceptance was the success of the open universities.

Open universities can be seen as the most advanced stage yet in the evolution of the concept of a university. One might trace this evolution from the residential universities of the nineteenth century to the introduction of non-residential full-time programmes late in the last century, to the introduction of part-time night-time courses in this century, followed by the creation of the distance teaching universities in the 1970s.

Open universities do not have students in residence, neither do they have full-time day-time students, nor even part-time night-time students. They place their students at home or, as in the Chinese system, at work. They are universities of a nation (Universidad Nacional de Educación a Distancia) or of a state (Fernuniversität-Gesamthochschule in Hagen), not of a city like Oxford, Paris or Bologna. Gone are the lecture rooms, tutorial rooms, the university library, laboratories for student research and facilities for the student community.

These universities present the most radical challenge yet to the idea of a university as enunciated by von Humboldt, Newman, Arnold or Jaspers.

Newman (1852; 1929) saw the university as a place where scholars came together for the purposes of learning and argued that if a practical end had to be assigned to a university course it was that of training good members of society: 'its art is the art of social life, and its end is fitness for the world'. His view was that the task of the university was to turn out an elite people who are educated in a broad sense, who are not just specialists but who have been enabled by their time at a university to see how their specialism may be brought into ... effective relation with informed general intelligence' (O'Hear, 1989). More recently Jaspers (1989) claimed that the university is a community of scholars and students engaged in the task of seeking truth.

Students who get their degrees from an open university cannot be said to be 'enabled by their time at a university' as they may never have been there except for the graduation ceremony and the concept of a 'community of scholars and students engaged in' a task in a distance learning system is really only a metaphor.

The idea of education

Further difficulties for the distance education theorist and for the relationship of distance education to the Great Tradition arise when the theory and practice of distance education are brought into juxtaposition with ideas from the influential positions on teaching and learning of the

University of London School of Education group led by R.S. Peters, Hirst and Oakeshott.

In a well-known passage R. Peters tells us that 'at the culminating stages of education there is little distinction between teacher and taught: they are both participating in the shared experience of exploring a common world' (1972:97). Learning is explained as a conversation or group experience in which there is 'intersubjectivity' between teacher and learner. Oakeshott carries this onwards by asking how does a person learn style, a personal idiom, honesty in research, willingness to submit cherished ideas to confrontation? His answer is that much of this is implanted unobtrusively in the manner in which information is conveyed, in a tone of voice. Much of this kind of dimension for Oakeshott (1967) can only be learned in the presence of one who has the qualities to be learned.

The essential feature of distance education is, however, that the teaching acts are separated in time and space from the learning acts and that the learning materials are offered to students one, five or ten years after they were developed and to students all over a country or overseas.

If the position of Peters and his group has validity, if the teaching-learning relationship is, indeed, basically a group experience then the establishment of a theoretical justification for claiming it can take place at a distance is crucial.

Research issues

The study of distance education

It is the role of the study of distance education to provide clarification of these questions of the theoretical underpinnings of distance education, especially at university degree level.

Moore (1985) guessed that the study of distance education had reached the level of development that the field of the study of adult education had reached thirty years previously. This is a useful yardstick, probably not too far wide of the mark.

Within the discipline education there are many fields of study. Some of these fields of teaching and research are usually considered to be essential for a faculty of education: educational psychology, history of education, philosophy of education, educational sociology. Some were more popular in the past than they are today: comparative education in the 1950s or curriculum theory in the 1980s. Some, like special education, are in vogue today. Some fields like educational administration, distance education or adult education are more specialised and may not be found in many universities. As yet there are teaching departments of distance education and research centres in distance education at few universities.

In an earlier article Moore (1973) set out the agenda for the field of study that came to be known as distance education: describing and defining the field; discriminating between the various components of this field; identifying the critical elements of the various forms of teaching and learning; building a theoretical framework that would embrace this whole area of education.

Today one can chronicle progress in the realisation of these requirements. Clarification of terminology was the work of the 1970s and 'distance education' emerged as the favoured term from the plethora of descriptors previously used for this form of education which included 'home study', 'correspondence education', 'teaching at a distance', external studies' and many more. Precision of definition was the work of the early 1980s. Great benefits for the field resulted from solving the problems of terminology and definition — energies that were formerly channelled into terminological cul-de-sacs were refocused into research in a field of study that was gaining cohesion. Better delineation of the field of study occurred in the late 1980s with scholars no longer wandering from distance education into related but disparate fields of study like educational technology or adult education or computing.

Taught degrees in the subject distance education arrived in the 1990s with a renewed interest in theoretical formulation. But the general consensus was that the theoretical underpinnings of a form of education that purported to provide a complete system of education from enrolment to examination and graduation, equal in quality but parallel to that of conventional schools, colleges and especially universities, was still unacceptably fragile.

Open learning, distance education, educational technology

A contributor to this fragility has been the failure of the field of distance education to define its area and its achievements, especially when contrasted with similar but different areas of provision or fields or research, notably 'open learning' and 'educational technology'.

In the book *The distance teaching universities* (1982), Rumble and I argued that 'distance teaching universities' was the correct title for universities which taught only at a distance rather than 'open universities'. The influence, however, of the Open University of the United Kingdom at Milton Keynes proved decisive and a series of distance universities chose to label themselves 'open', the most recent being the Open University of Tanzania (1993), the Open University of Bangladesh (1994) and no less than seven open universities in India, either recently inaugurated or in process of foundation. The term was continued much less successfully with the Open Tech (much hyped but short lived), the Open College, an attempt to institutionalise open programmes at further education level, and the Open Polytechnic, which had to be hastily renamed as it was founded at the time that the UK government was phasing out polytechnics.

The trouble with 'open' institutions is that peoples' judgments vary as to what is 'open' and what is 'closed'. Unlike many other distance education institutions the Open University has closed enrolment dates, closed assignment cut-off dates and compulsory residential schools that close it off from many. Historians describe the dialogue of Plato as an open didactic structure, yet Popper (1960) launched a bitter attack on him as the enemy of openness.

The field of educational technology deals with the use of technology in education both conventional and at a distance. From many points of view it predates the scientific development of distance education and goes back to programmed learning. Its assessment of the effectiveness of new technologies for schools, colleges and universities is a vital contribution to the development of distance education, but even those educational technologists who work in distance universities have largely failed to identify with research on distance education.

The perfect teaching machine

It is now seventy years since educational technologists set out in pursuit of the perfect teaching machine, perhaps the most striking challenge to the Great Tradition. This would be a machine that would either replace the teacher totally or at least reduce the teacher to a role of a mere facilitator to the programmes of the machine.

Most analysts would, with Hawkridge (1976), begin with Pressey's educational testing machine developed in 1926 and his prophecy that 'a revolution in education is about to dawn, bringing great benefits of more effective and more efficient learning' (Pressey, 1927). Pressey was followed by Skinner who in 1954 produced programmed learning machines 'to perform most of the functions the teacher could not perform, as well as some of those the teacher could' (Skinner, 1954). The

1960s and 1970s saw the investment of enormous sums of money in ceaseless efforts to produce the universally adaptable teaching machine.

The efforts of technologists to produce machines that would replace teachers were linked to prophecies that the latest technological developments would empty the schools and colleges of the world. The best known is probably that by Edison in 1913:

> The motion picture is the great educator of the poorer people. It incites their imagination by bringing the whole world before their eyes. It sets spectators thinking and raises their standard of living. Books will soon be obsolete in the public schools. Scholars will be instructed through the eye.

Edison's forecast that the cinematograph would transform schools and universities was followed by forecasts that programmed learning would empty schools and colleges in the 1950s and similar forecasts by the futurists about computers in the 1970s. From time to time distance educators join in these rash forecasts, with special references to the ills of conventional education that distance education can correct and writing in particularly harsh terms of the problems of the university lecture as a didactic strategy.

Defenders of conventional values have not been slow to rebut these superficial proposals by distance educators and educational technologists. Boshier (1985:139) is particularly withering:

> A few years ago 'non-traditional learning' was touted as a mechanism to democratise education. Today ministers of education are happily hacking at 'traditional' institutions which are easily replaced by distance education. There is a vast irony in this because distance education was supposed to help democratise educational processes; few anticipated that it would be a weapon used to beat the heads of institutions where learners and teachers have the temerity to gather together to learn in groups.

Conclusion

1995 and beyond

A breathtaking array of technologies already developed by the telecommunications industry is now ready for implementation in educational programmes. These technologies include: universal mobile telephony, satellite virtual classrooms, universal personal telephony, fibre-to-the-local-loop, two-way video codec systems, videoconferencing to the desktop, broadband ISDN, multimedia to the home. The didactic possibilities of these technologies are immense and within years they will come on line and wait to be harnessed by distance education.

The challenges these developments pose to both conventional universities and to distance systems are also immense, as it is already clear that the technology has already been developed to provide two-way video, two-way audio lecturing and tutoring to the student's personal desktop — whether at work or at home. Some (Smith and Kelly, 1987) have suggested that these new telecommunications developments will lead to a fusing of distance and conventional education and to a blurring of the boundaries between them. Others have claimed that these new technologies, all focused on keeping the student away from school or university and from whatever vestiges of the Great Tradition that remain, will increase the divergences between off-campus and face-to-face provision. It seems clear that it would put unfair burdens on normal teachers and lecturers, whose focus is the learning of the student who comes to school, to expect them to become experts in an ever increasing array of home-based telecommunications.

For the field of distance education there are three further caveats as the next century approaches. The first comes from Wedemeyer's (1981) ideal for distance education that 'it should be available any time, anywhere there are students or only one student'. This has been a touchstone for access and quality in distance education for the last two decades. Should this now be abandoned and students forced to travel to electronic classrooms for their videoconferences and satellite lectures? Whether these are one-way video or two-way video many of the new telecommunications possibilities compel the student to travel to the electronic centre at a fixed time on a fixed day, thus reintroducing the timetabling of learning that Wedemeyer was so anxious to avoid.

Secondly, does one have to be rich to learn? As the distance education literature focuses more and more on new technological developments, none of which can be claimed to be didactically superior to any other medium as the classic studies of Dubin and Taveggia (1968), Schramm (1977) and Clark (1983) show clearly enough, but most of which are costlier than the technology that went before, what will happen to distance education's much vaunted cost-effectiveness? Much of the success of this form of education in the developed and, certainly, in the developing world is due to the economies of scale of reproducing in great numbers cheaply produced, but didactically sound, printed materials. Not only does one not have to be rich to learn in a distance programme, neither does one have to enrol in a system filled with expensive technologies if one wants to learn successfully.

Finally distance education brings with it, it has been said, many of the benefits and dangers of the industrialisation and of the privatisation of education. The technology is already in place, or nearly in place, to teach face-to-face at a distance to the home. This home of the future will, in many cases, have an integrated audiovisual terminal comprising a video display and sound reproduction unit with voice-activated controls using sophisticated speech recognition software, with CD drive, cable/satellite terminal, videophone and computer module. The dangers of privatisation of student learning may be dramatic and the role of the Great Tradition and related philosophies may need to be restated.

Distance education solutions

As the search for educational solutions for the next century progresses it is coming to be recognised that the field of distance education research can make valuable contributions to research on education in general as well as to its own limited area. The reason for this is that distance education is a separate form of education and can approach problems of research with a perspective that is different from and, in some cases, impossible for researchers in the other fields of educational scholarship. Added to this is the consideration that the variables in a range of research situations can be more distinct in a distance education context because the student is separated in time and space from the teacher and is also separated from other learners on the same programme. Three recent developments are briefly referred to here: streaming; very large systems, formative assessment and feedback.

Streaming is one of the persistent problems of face-to-face education deriving from the heterogeneous study backgrounds, the differing learning styles and the varying abilities of each individual in the learning group. In distance education attempts (Vertecchi, 1993) can be put in place to address this characteristic problem of conventional educational provision. In distance education one can envisage the development of a specific educational strategy of offering each student an individualised course corresponding to his/her characteristics using personalised learning paths for each student. In practice the process is computerised thus: first, the learning objectives are accurately defined; for each objective corresponding cognitive prerequisites are determined; all students are tested for the prerequisites; the learning path is then subdivided into segments; each segment is written in versions differing in level or perspective; the results of the prerequisites test show which version of each segment is most suitable for each student. The operations described in the last step are computerised and the textual variants and the data from the students' responses to the tests are stored in the computer. The computer then proceeds to the production of an individual text for each student.

Secondly, research in distance education has shown how this form of education can accommodate very large numbers of students. Educational politicians (Coombs, 1985) have shown the pressing needs of educational provision, especially in developing countries. In many cases the need is for institutions enrolling hundreds of thousands rather than tens of thousands of students. It is fair to say that in many parts of the world governments no longer have the resources and their taxpayers no longer have the money to build buildings for hundreds of thousands of students. Very large distance education institutions, however, are not uncommon.

Statistics published by the Open University of the United Kingdom in 1994 for the 25th anniversary celebrations of the reception of its Royal Charter showed that it had nearly 140,000 students. In Spain the Universidad Nacional de Educación a Distancia had at least as many. In France the Centre National d'Education à Distance, founded for children in 1939 when Hitler invaded, has grown to 350,000 students in 107 countries in courses at all levels from primary schooling to postgraduate university studies. In Thailand the Sukhothai Thammatirat Open University has 450,000 students and the world's largest distance university system, the Central Chinese Radio and Television University, has 850,000 in 1994. The study of very large distance systems, how they function and what contributes to the didactic success of systems enrolling over 100,000 students annually, is an important area for distance education research and one which cannot properly be carried out by researchers in other fields like departments of adult education or institutes of educational technology. Analyses of such systems are needed by educational planners and governments in both developed and developing countries.

Modern technology harnessed to distance education can turn former weaknesses of this form of education into new strengths. A case in point is formative evaluation and feedback. Classic distance education research studies (Rekkedal, 1983) had shown how students' learning could be damaged by delayed feedback. Today it is possible for students enrolled all over Europe in a distance university to complete specially designed assignments at any time of day or night, any day of the year, and to send them to the university's computer which will correct the assignment, print out a personalised analysis of the student's strengths or weaknesses and send it immediately back to the student.

Distance education, and especially distance education at university level, has been presented in this chapter as a form of education which in its evolution from the days of the Industrial Revolution to the present shared few of the characteristics of the Great Tradition, but which, of itself, is not inimical to it.

References

Boshier, R. (1985). Book review. *The International Review of Education*, 31, 1, 139-40.

Boyd, W. and King, E. (1969). *The history of western education*. London: Black.

Clark, R. (1983). Reconsidering research on learning from media. *Review of Educational Research*, 53, 4, 445-459.

Coombs, P. (1985). *The world crisis in education*. Oxford: Oxford University Press.

Devlin, T. (1993). Distance training. In *Distance education: new perspectives* (eds. K. Harry, M. John, and D. Keegan), pp. 254-268. London: Routledge.

Dubin, R. and Taveggia, T. (1968). *The teaching learning paradox: Comparative analysis of college teaching methods*. Eugene: University of Oregon.

Edison, T. (1913). The evolution of the motion picture. *The New York Dramatic Mirror*, 9 July 1913, 24-5.

Hawkridge, D. (1976). Next year, Jerusalem, the rise of educational technology. *British Journal of Educational Technology*, 7, 1, 7-30.

Jaspers, K. (1989). Quoted by K. Wilson in 'The pattern, range and purpose of higher education: a moral perspective'. In *Higher Education into the 1990s* (eds. C. Bell and H. Eggins), pp. 38-50. London: SRHE.

O'Hear, A. (1989). The university as a civilizing force. In *Higher Education into the 1990s* (eds. C. Ball and H. Eggins). London: SRHE.

Moore, M. (1973). Toward a theory of independent learning and teaching. *Journal of Higher Education*, 44, 661-79.

Moore, M. (1985). Some observations on current research on distance education. *Epistolo didaktika*, 1, 35-62.

Newman, J. (1852; 1929). *The idea of a university*. London: Longman Green.

Oakeshott, M. (1967). Learning and teaching. In *The concept of Education* (ed. R. Peters). London: Routledge and Kegan Paul.

Peters, O. (1994). *The industrialization of teaching and learning: Otto Peters on distance education*. London: Routledge.

Peters, R. (1972). Education as initiation. In *Philosophical Analysis and Education* (ed. R. Achambault). London: Routledge and Kegan Paul.

Popper, K. (1960). *The OpenSsociety and its Enemies*. London: Macmillan.

Pressey, S. (1927). A machine for automatic teaching of drill material. *School and Society*, 25.

Rekkedal, T. (1984). The written assignments in correspondence education. Effects of reducing turn-around time. An experimental study. *Distance Education*, 4, 2, 231-252.

Rumble, G. and Keegan, D. (1982). General characteristics of the distance teaching universities. In *The Distance Teaching Universities* (eds. G. Rumble and K. Harry), pp. 204-224. London: Croom Helm.

Schramm, W. (1977). *Big Media, Little Media*. London: Sage.

Skinner, B. (1954). The science of learning and the art of teaching. *Harvard Educational Review*, 24, 2, 101-123.

Smith, K. (1979). *External Studies at New England: A Silver Jubilee Review*. Armidale: UNE.

Smith, P. and Kelly, M. (eds.) (1987). *Distance Education and the Mainstream*. London: Croom Helm.

Vertecchi, B. (1993). Structural analysis of distance education. In *Theoretical Principles of Distance Education* (ed. D. Keegan), pp. 152-164. London: Routledge.

Wedemeyer, C. (1981). *Learning at the Back Door*. Madison: University of Wisconsin.

Wiltshire, H. (1956). The great tradition in university adult education. *Adult Education*, XXIX, 2. Reprinted in *The Spirit and the Form* (ed. A. Rogers, 1976). Department of Adult Education, University of Nottingham.

Adult Education and 'Overseas Development'

David J. Alexander

I intend in this chapter to analyse the current context and meaning of 'development' in what is termed the 'New World Order' (NWO), its effects on curriculum and adult educators and the implications for resistance and a democratic future. I will focus on Zambia's experience as, although each country and region is different, it epitomises many of the human, economic, cultural and political problems faced in much of Sub-Saharan Africa. In addition Zambia is of major interest in the context of this book because it has one of the strongest trade union organisations on the African continent which, as a social movement with a significant workers' education programme, made a major contribution to the political and historic shift to multi-party 'democracy' in the elections of October 1991. I emphasise socio-economic discussion of Zambia in the context of the NWO because it is necessary for adult educators to position themselves and their selection of curricula in the evidence of economic, human, ecological and political crisis and the blatancy of imperial domination and military power.

The 'New Right' announces the demise of imperialism at a time when capital is expanding through national boundaries and states, expansion and restructuring always being the imperative of capital, and requires its collaborator imperialism more than ever before. The 'Third World' no longer exists except as an object of occasional virtuous charity, a cheap venue for tedious package holidays, and a source of bright commercial ideas for 'ethnic' fashion, food, and interesting stories and tunes. We are one world now.

The poor are always with us consisting of the majority of the population of the South, an increasing underclass in the West and East together with hordes of refugees and economic migrants to be controlled in the interest of the international division of labour by appropriate immigration laws. Language is important. This majority are the 'donors' of aid not the recipients and suffer the indignity of having their land, natural resources and labour pushed into forms of development which make them poor through, for example, the net export of food and other primary commodities at low prices in order to pay off external debt at high interest rates when they themselves are hungry and dying. They subsidise the 'democracy' of Organisation for Economic Cooperation and Development (OECD) countries, which function to integrate the labour of the poor into a changing and refined strategy of global exploitation.

At the same time this 'democratic' culture seeks to obscure its predatory violence in the language of the peace dividend, liberal democracy, pluralism, transparency, good governance, aid and the relief of famine, a new world order of freedom and the flexibility of labour. All other subordinate, residual and oppositional cultures and languages are dismissed as deviant, hysterical, whinging, 'minority' views of the world. These are the subjugated majority narratives, histories, languages, and words of 'feminists', 'green' people, environmentalists, trade unionists, urban workers and rural peasants, the unemployed, socialists and neo-Marxists. 'These people' also include adult educators who do not seek a liberal neutral balance, an accommodation, a strategic compliance, or a broker's role in the work of education but a search for the truth and for its diffusion. Democratic adult educators oppose the 'New World Order' with a curriculum of political literacy and a language of hope and possibility based in reclaimed histories and present knowledges which have and do form the basis of resistance and opposition to the violence of imposed world knowledge systems. Dependency in the creation and diffusion of knowledge may be the deepest dependency of all: 'cultural hegemony is characterised not only by what it includes but by what it excludes, renders marginal, deems inferior and makes invisible' (Fasheh, 1992). The hegemonic project of the 'New Right' is to remoralise society and education on the basis of individual free choice in the market-place, to centralise power and to reduce active mutual citizenship to individual consumer rights.

We have reached a point of historic crisis. The forces generated by the techno-scientific economy are now great enough to destroy the environment, the material foundations of human life. The structures of human societies themselves, including even some of the social foundations of the capitalist economy are on the point of being destroyed by the erosion of what we have inherited from the human past. Our world risks both explosion and implosion. It must change.

Hobsbawm (1994)

The notion that these developments, expressed in the South and Eastern Europe by Structural Adjustment Programmes (SAP) imposed by the International Monetary Fund (IMF) and the World Bank (WB) whose officials are accountable only to their dominant shareholders in the USA and other G7 countries, are confined to 'overseas' countries and 'others' is of course flawed. In curricular terms the competency movement and technicist reform in education designed to produce an efficient, flexible and cheap work-force, expressed in the South for example by 'The Framework for Action to meet Basic Learning Needs' (World Conference on Education for All, 1990), must be located in the global context of the oppressive imperialism of the 'New World Order' (see Torres, 1991). I do not use the term 'oppressive imperialism' as an outworn slogan but to emphasise that it continues to exist and is renamed the 'democracy of the market-place'. The collapse of authoritarian communist states does not mean that 'democracy' and capitalism have triumphed in the interests of the majority of the world's population. A study of the rapacious and brutal human, social, political and economic effects of SAPs provides overwhelming evidence of the drive for power by currently dominant economic forces which are ultimately supported by military coercion. These programmes and the dismantling of public education, health and social programmes in so many countries of Sub-Saharan Africa and elsewhere, and the implementation of the obscenely termed 'cost-sharing' programmes in these areas which mean that the poor can no longer benefit and as a consequence die painfully and invisibly in their millions, are to be seen as part of the world-wide casualisation of labour and anti-labour policies. These are linked with industry and employer-controlled Human Resource Development (HRD)/Human Resource Management (HRM) approaches to education and training which are based on an ahistorical and depthless language of deceit and moral despair and the promotion of political, economic and cultural illiteracy.

This neo-liberal economic and cultural programme has structural, institutional and ideological dimensions. Public issues are transmuted into 'personal troubles' and social pathology. It is perhaps, in the context of this book, important to recognise continuities between current neo-liberal hegemony and the 'ideology of individualism' which permeated the tradition of English liberal adult education (see for example Keddie, 1980 and Griffin, 1983).

> In many ways, the elisions of the latter can now be seen to have prepared the ground for the incursion of the former. And we have to recognise the unwitting collusion of many adult and community educators in the present conjunction of pedagogical individuation with ideological atomisation consequent upon 'new' right intervention.
>
> Alexander and Martin (1995)

The liberal tradition was exported via university departments of extra-mural studies to the colonies from the 1940s onwards. The present neo-liberal programme deeply affects 'aid' and its educational and economic uses by the British Overseas Development Administration under the current guidance of Baroness Chalker and her professional allies in the establishment of English adult education still wholeheartedly engaged in philanthropic deceit and the diffusion of 'useful' rather than 'really useful' knowledge. These are the 'donors' of the rotted and decadent roots of liberalism deprived of the morality of Mill's ghost.

Motives are further concealed by notions of 'efficiency', predetermined educational outcomes, technical rationality, and performance indicators which are driven by a concern to transfer control away from students and teachers towards the interests of employers, business and the central state acting as an agent of international capital. The doctrinally non-doctrinaire, pseudo-positivist, objective, rational scientific approach to human affairs is unscientific, concealing purposes which are destructive of intellectual acuity, critical intelligence, communality, common welfare, the essential equality of human being and democracy (see Inglis, 1988).

One significant example of the effects of these approaches has been the distortions and cruelties inflicted by politically correct 'Women in Development' (WID) income generation programmes, many of which have resulted in the further exploitation of women, and do not question the nature of 'development' itself as envisaged in the 'New World Order'. Any economic gains made were largely wiped out by unfavourable commodity prices and gains in critical understanding diminished through control of curricula and research agendas by Northern white middle class women, although resistance to these is developing. The significance of questioning the nature of development is emphasised by Marjorie Mbilinyi (1992:18):

> structural adjustment policies negated most of the positive achievements of WID programmes. They seek to reverse 'decolonisation' policies, lower the real wages of workers, and reduce the real cash returns of small producers including women, so as to create 'cheap' labour for 'capital'. Resources have been shifted away from small scale growers, including women, to the owners of large farms and plantations — primarily trans-national corporations and both foreign and national entrepreneurs.

A significant response to the NWO on the 'left' in Britain is to embrace a 'new individualism' in the context of a globalised economy and cultural order and the dynamics of the 'free market' which are presented as inevitable.

> The new individualism is a mixture of positives and negatives. In the increasingly global cosmopolitan world which is the context of our daily activities, we all have to construct our lives more actively than ever was the case before ... To put things simply, our lives are less and less lived as fate.
>
> Giddens (1994:38)

Giddens does not equate the 'new individualism' with the self seeking morality of the market-place but it may be useful to locate individual choice and the diminution of fate, a useful word to replace economic and structural causation and the explanatory power of history, in a Zambian reality. Zambia, together with other Sub-Saharan African countries, is experiencing an economic and human crisis of devastating proportions. The economic crisis is not to be seen only in terms of structural problems, chronic shortage of foreign exchange, adverse terms of trade and increasing indebtedness but in terms of much deeper human crisis affecting morale, the basic capacity to regenerate the economy, the social fabric and the knowledge and cultural base. There are rapidly growing levels of unemployment and underemployment, absolute and relative poverty and a worsening and skewed income distribution which are having appalling effects on the quality of life, health, literacy and education. The major fear of Zambian educators is that even if they can manage to expand the educational system for children and adults, malnutrition and ill-health will be destructive of learning capacities. The educators themselves are malnourished and often sick due to wages which cannot feed or house them and their families, the introduction of charges for public health services, and the lack of medical supplies and drugs.

Zambia has been undergoing IMF and World Bank programmes of increasing intensity and conditionality since the 1970s. The need to reduce poverty is:

> more than a matter of economic good sense and political expediency. It rests on the ethic of human solidarity, of concern for others, of human response to human suffering.
>
> Kalyalya and Muuka (1994)

It was conservatively estimated in 1991 that 54% of Zambia's 7.9 million population was 'very poor' (76% rural and 29% urban) and 14% 'poor' (12% rural and 17% urban). Poverty has increased considerably since 1991 with more stringent implementation of Zambia's SAP (see note).

The nature of the 'new individualism' in a cosmopolitan global economy, the extent of choice, the possibility of choosing an identity and lifestyle, the joys of difference and the excited celebration of postmodern fragments, may in Zambia be discerned in terms of 'coping mechanisms', strategies and skills which the poor, now at least 71% of the population (Central Statistical Office, 1993), have had to adopt to generate income for survival as a result of continued economic recession and the negative impacts of Zambia's current SAP, widely known in Lusaka's townships and bottle stores as the 'Stomach Adjustment Programme'.

Coping mechanisms and skills utilised by the urban poor and vulnerable in Zambia

(Adapted from Kalyalya and Muuka, 1994: 23-25)

(a)   Change in eating habits due to high food costs and low or absent income base — eat not three but one or at best two meals a day.

(b)   Increasing absenteeism from school by children forced to engage in income generation including petty trading and thieving.

(c)   Unprecedented incidence of begging for money and food. Most of those involved in open, direct begging in public places are disabled, many of them blind, adults and young children. There has been over the past ten years an unprecedented increase in the number of street children, indicating massive cultural breakdown in the face of imposed poverty. Most blind beggars are adults and quite elderly and are usually guided by children between seven and twelve years of age.

(d) Increased petty street vending and trading.

(e) 'Kaloba' — informal credit schemes. Short-term unofficial lending of on the spot cash at interest rates of between 50% and 150%.

(f) Increased prostitution by the female poor to raise money for food and basic necessities for themselves, their parents and/or their children.

(g) Diversification and deepening of informal income generating activities such as the crushing and selling of stones by women, especially in Lusaka.

(h) Illicit beer and spirit brewing.

(i) Some incidence of returning to home rural areas.

(j) Increased crime, including aggravated robbery and rape.

(k) Increased reliance on ing'anga (traditional healers) for medical attention due to introduction of fees in formal health institutions as part of World Bank and IMF induced subsidy removals.

(l) Increasing use of backyard gardens as a source of vegetables for consumption and sale.

(m) Increase in open gambling in the streets, often involving passers-by.

(n) Increased street crime.

Coping mechanisms and skills utilised by the rural poor and vulnerable in Zambia

(a) Selling livestock to raise money to make ends meet.

(b) More widespread and intensified illicit beer and spirit brewing.

(c) Increased sale of vegetables and other farm produce often resulting in malnutrition.

(d)   Increased production of charcoal for sale as fuel in urban centres which is environmentally destructive.

(e)   Gathering wild fruits for household consumption and sale.

(f)   Increased fishing.

(g)   Looking for jobs in urban areas.

(h)   Casual work on commercial farms.

(i)   Food for work projects — work fare.

(j)   Increased reliance on ing'anga.

(k)   Petty thieving.

These represent the rich array of the choices, strategies and skills of the 'new individualism' in a Zambian context where street children, for example, were unheard of until ten years ago. Kalyalya and Muuka (1994: 25) comment,

> The above coping mechanisms by both the urban and rural poor are, of course, unsustainable, at worst highly inadequate in halting the poor's slippage into deeper poverty.

Zambia became independent in October 1964 as a relatively prosperous country in Sub-Saharan Africa, though with inequitable income distribution. The structure of the economy has changed little since independence being largely dependent on copper and lacking in diversification. Perhaps most important for the regeneration of the economy, human welfare and food security, has been the neglect of the agricultural sector, despite its vast potential, and of small and peasant farmers, which has meant a failure to achieve sustained self-sufficiency in food production, an over-emphasis on maize at the expense of other basic food crops, rural immiseration for the majority and massive urban migration. The United National Independence Party (UNIP), in power until October 1991, did not address this neglect and continued the colonial policy of viewing agriculture as a means of providing cheap food for the towns with correspondingly low prices for small rural producers and unfavourable rural/urban terms of trade. Women frequently suffer most at a time when female-headed households are increasing rapidly to well over 60% in some rural areas (Central Statistical Office, 1993: 39). These women may have a hoe, less than a hectare of land, no credit, no collateral, no draught power, no agricultural extension advice and no labour except their own and what exists in their household of perhaps four younger and two or three older dependants. Well over 200,000 small peasant households are headed by women due to rural poverty and male migration to the towns despite the lack of employment. Family breakdown, malnutrition and sickness, compounded by real cuts in public expenditure in the health and social services, are rife. The position has been worsened by recent moves to 'liberalise' the economy and small farmers are being offered appallingly low and exploitative prices by private traders for their produce.

Zambia's dependence on copper, a monocultural position typical of many Sub-Saharan African and other economically poor countries, make it particularly vulnerable to external world market 'shocks'. Zambia has been dependent on copper for 93-95% of its export earnings and for about 40-45% of Gross Domestic Product. Despite warnings from Zambian and other economists from the late 1960s, critical debate on this dependence did not impact upon policy makers, despite their continual rhetoric concerning the importance of rural development, until 1973. The large contribution of the copper industry to government revenue and foreign exchange earnings enabled Zambia to expand its public education, health and other public services and the educational achievements were enormous. Until Independence, child, adult and youth education had been neglected. The educational legacy of British colonialism was that in 1964 one million adults (two thirds of the then adult population) were illiterate or sub-literate. The great majority of the rural population had never been to school. Only 15% of men and 3% of women had more than four years primary education. Only 1,200 African Zambians had obtained secondary school certificates. The total number of African Zambian university graduates was just over 100. Nor, due to the racism practised by white trade unions and the policy of the colonial administration which treated Zambian workers as rural tribesmen and migrant labour, did Zambia possess a stable, skilled, industrial work-force based on copper and secondary industry. By 1975 approximately 86% of primary age children (7-14) were in school, although there was a substantial push-out at Grade 4 due to lack of places particularly in the rural areas. However, only 23% of primary school leavers could find places in secondary school. There was a small Department of Adult Education in the Ministry of Education; literacy programmes were run by the Department of Community Development; a small university extension programme on a largely liberal model was in operation and there were significantly strong developments in workers' education run by the Zambia Congress of

Trade Unions (ZCTU) and its affiliated unions (Alexander, 1983 and 1990). This workers' education programme, its curriculum firmly independent of state control, together with the labour movement of which it was an organic part, were to have a highly significant role to play in the removal in October 1991, after 27 years of power, of President Kaunda and the UNIP government. I will argue that as a critically conscious social movement organised labour may still have an important role in domestic political development and in resisting the depredations of the 'New World Order' despite its current difficulties.

The first of the massive external shocks to the vulnerable Zambian economy came in 1973 with the world oil crisis. Zambia has no known oil reserves, is land-locked and entirely dependent on foreign supplies. The second came in 1974 and 1975 with the sharp fall in copper prices. The oil crisis meant an increased import bill and the fall in copper prices a large reduction in foreign exchange earnings to pay for it. In turn this resulted in a major reduction of necessary essential imports and a fall in average capacity utilisation in industry from 65% in 1974 to 30% in 1984 (Muuka, 1993).

In the belief and hope that copper prices would recover, Zambia began to borrow and accumulated foreign debt until the present disastrous situation of indebtedness. It embarked in 1973 on its first stabilisation package, obtaining an IMF standby agreement loan to help cushion the impact of the fall in copper prices. Prices did not recover, successful diversification of the economy did not occur, and the neglect of agriculture was not remedied leading to the current position in which the IMF and World Bank, with the enthusiastic co-operation of the present Movement for Multi-Party Democracy (MMD) government, can impose their Structural Adjustment Programme (SAP) with increasingly strict conditionalities. Zambia's per capita income has declined rapidly during the 1980s and 1990s. In 1985 the World Bank reclassified Zambia from a low/middle income country to a low income country. By 1987 GNP per capita had fallen to US $250. Today Zambia is one of the world's 47 'least developed' countries despite its involvement with IMF and WB 'Stabilisation' and 'Structural Adjustment Programmes' over a period of 21 years. A former World Bank official takes the view that Zambia's difficulties were exacerbated by World Bank lending during the 1970s which did not emphasise a better allocation of resources to agriculture (King, 1991).

The effects of adverse international terms of trade during the 1980s and 1990s which far outweigh the significance of 'aid' from North to South, inappropriate World Bank, IMF and bilateral loans, projects and advice and protectionist measures adopted by the 'industrialised' countries (for example the US Farm Act, 1986) and the politics, economics and marketing opportunities of 'famine' together with internal problems, have led to the present situation of indebtedness, stagnation and frequent 'stagflation'. The purposes and effects of the IMF and WB 'stabilisation' and SAPs are by now well documented (see for example Cornia et al. (eds.), 1992; Adedeji (ed.), 1993; Adepoju (ed.), 1993; Rau, 1991; Graham-Brown, 1991; Muuka, 1993; ILO Report of the Director-General, January 1994). SAPs and the scale of human and social effects differ from country to country but have the same broad themes. Their stated purposes include the encouragement of non-traditional exports; reduction of balance of payments and budget deficits; diversification of the economy to make it less vulnerable to external shocks; eventual resumption of higher rates of growth and the reduction of foreign debt.

SAPs are partly based on neo-classical 'growth-first' models similar to those of the 1950s and 1960s (Adepoju, 1993) with an increased reliance on the 'free market' and reduced state intervention. These are mirrored in education by HRD/HRM approaches, similar to the discredited 'man-power planning' models and incremental capital output ratio theories of the same period using different languages and techniques and most recently dressed up as a moral concern for the centrality of 'human development' (United Nations Development Programme, 1990).

This is an unfashionable argument and even more unfashionable language but it is time to be unfashionable — the reasons for the continuation and savage refinement of these programmes into the 1990s despite massive and mounting evidence of failure in terms of the interests, purposes, values and material well-being of the majority are to be related to the nature of the social relations of production and the international division of labour in the current restructuring of capital.

Means of implementing the purposes of SAPs which are imposed as conditions for further loans include:

(a) reductions in government expenditure through deep cuts in the civil service, public investment, expenditure on education, health, social services and subsidies, including in Zambia the abolition of subsidy to the basic food-stuff, maize-meal;

(b) expansion of foreign earnings through devaluation of local currencies and incentives to companies and farmers to increase exports although the latter are accompanied by elimination of producer input subsidies such as those on fertilisers;

(c)   the elimination of state and parastatal industries through privatisation;

(d)   a general wage freeze and anti trade union environment;

(e)   removal of legal restriction on private entrepreneurship and abolition of state enterprises and monopolies in both production and marketing;

(f)   giving preference to the private sector using 'free market' prices to influence production and consumption;

(g)   trade liberalisation, removal of import restrictions, domestic industry protection, and price controls;

(h)   financial deregulation.

These measures have resulted in increased malnutrition, poverty, unemployment and underemployment in both formal and informal sectors, the chronic deterioration of education, health and social services and the collapse of transport and marketing infrastructures. In Africa for example the share of education and health expenditure fell from 25% in 1986 to 19% in 1988 and the position has deteriorated since then in many countries including Zambia. The rural and urban poor have suffered devastating effects. Health and education charges have been introduced. Trade liberalisation in Zambia has resulted in the collapse of major sectors of the manufacturing industry which are becoming traders rather than producers (Muuka, 1993). The measures have contributed to even greater income inequality and the concentration or wealth in the hands of the top 5% of the population. Partly due to the emphasis on exports rather than on production for the domestic market and chaotic marketing and pricing, food security has not been achieved.

Zambia's population is approximately 8.5 million and growing at 3.2% per annum. The labour force is approximately 4 million and the percentage employed in the formal sector declined from 26.6% to 15.4% between 1975 and 1988 and to 9.8% in 1990.

The government's *Economic Report for 1993* (Office of the President, National Commission for Development Planning, January 1994: 26) shows declining trends of employment between 1992 and 1993 and comments that:

> The current economic restructuring process seems to have a negative impact on formal employment in Zambia. In response to the changing economic environment, firms have continued to undertake

cost-saving measures including effecting labour cuts. It is apparent therefore that Zambia requires massive investment outlays to address the employment situation.

Employment in the government sector which includes most community, social and personal services is to be 'pruned'. Redundancy and retirement packages from the civil service are currently so low as to be almost non-existent with inflation running at 200%.

Policies aimed at reducing social and health services together with the abolition of subsidies show major effects between 1990 and 1992:

(a)   life expectancy at birth has been reduced from 54 to 45 years;

(b)   crude death rate per 1,000 has increased from 13 to 18;

(c)   infant mortality rate per 1,000 had increased from 76 to 113;

(d)   under-five mortality rate per 1,000 has increased from 122 to 202.

In 1990 the daily calorie supply as a percentage of requirements was 87% and only 25% of the population had access to safe drinking water in 1994. The 'liberalisation' and 'free market' measures which have been rapidly applied since 1992 have resulted in a further rapid deterioration of social conditions. Seshemani (1992: 125) commenting on the lack of adequate protection for vulnerable groups states:

> any further adverse impact on poverty and income inequality could convert the economic crisis in Zambia into a social catastrophe.

This has now occurred. Lack of food security and health provision is resulting in malnutrition, sickness and death on a scale never before experienced in Zambia. Seshemani (1992: 129) insists that a direct approach to the improvement of well-being is required and that to 'rely on policy which seeks to better the condition of the poor largely through the "trickle-down effect" of efficient growth is unacceptable'.

Zambia is facing a deepening debt crisis. One of the consequences of the SAP is deindustrialisation and an increased inability to service loans. Zambia's current internal debt stands at US$ 6.7 billion which is the equivalent of 700% of the country's export earnings.

> Every Zambian including newborn children owes US$ 800 or Zambian Kwacha 675,000. It is almost impossible for Zambia to pay with our declined real income levels and high unemployment. The overall picture of indebtedness in Zambia is alarming and

completely rules out raising the standards of living of the Zambian people which is about 40% of what it was in 1970. In short, what I am trying to hint at is the fact that the labour movement is now faced with more and greater challenges than ever before.

Alec Chirwa
Secretary General, Zambian Congress of Trade Unions
(August 1994)

45% of the debt is owed to multilateral creditors including the IMF and World Bank, 40% to bilateral creditors and the remainder to commercial banks and suppliers. The IMF and World Bank are much more interested in debt collection than in the economic welfare of countries they are supposed to be helping.

> Between 1983 and 1990 the Fund's [IMF] operations resulted in a net transfer of resources amounting to US$ 3.1 billion from Sub-Saharan Africa.
>
> Kapijimpanga (1994: 4)

Debt service reduces the capacity of the economy to regenerate and achieve sustainable economic adjustment. The preference of bilateral creditors, mainly OECD countries in the Paris Club, to reschedule debt on unfavourable terms followed by capitalised interest on non-concessional terms, has had negative effects in that they exacerbate balance of payments problems and reduce resources for domestic programmes including those for rebuilding infrastructure, education, health and other social and public services. Bilateral (country to country) aid is also being used to service multilateral debt which discourages individual countries from providing financial assistance.

> Moreover recently debt service has come to depend on balance of payments support from multilateral and bilateral agencies. However, this support is granted on condition that Zambia meets her debt obligations. This accentuates the problem as repayment of old debt begets new debt. In short, debt service has put the country in some kind of a vicious circle ... you have a debt so you borrow to finance it only to end up with a larger debt than before and this goes on ad infinitum.
>
> Kalyalya and Muuka (1994: 15-16)

Such analyses and the perceptions and evidence of Zambian trade unionists tell us much more about the economic realities and lives of people than World Bank and IMF officials and reports. These latter speak in the 1990s a new language of sustainable growth, ecological concern, investment in human resources, pious afterthoughts in the form of quite illusory safety nets for the poor and vulnerable run by community development workers who cannot themselves subsist on their wages. President Chiluba has stressed that measures would be taken to protect the poorest but despite projected expenditure in the Public Investment Programme 1992-95 (Office of the President, NCDP March 1992) the Social Action Programme 1990-93 (Republic of Zambia 1990) it is difficult to see how this protection can be effectively achieved (ICFTU, ZCTU, FES, 1992). For many the promised effect of economic reforms and efforts made to protect the poor from what we are told is the necessary price of economic success, and the need to reduce inflation will come too late. Tighter monetary and fiscal policies are being applied to further restrain budget deficits (Office of the President, Planning Division, 1992:2).

At a time of three-figure inflation, subsidies were abolished and prices decontrolled before any poverty alleviation measures were introduced. The Social Action Programme was merely added on to 'liberalisation' programmes rather than as an integral part. Poverty alleviation programmes are underfunded and severely dependent on donor support and non-governmental organisations. Alec Chirwa, Secretary-General, ZCTU, in a speech to women trade unionists in August 1994 remarked:

> In March 1993 I was appointed to the national Social Safety Net Co-ordinating Committee. To date we are still discussing how we are going to operate. Why? — There are no resources.
>
> Chirwa (1994)

The realities of concern for human development are reflected in the decline in real expenditure on education form ZK 249.5 million to ZK 131.2 million between 1984 and 1991. The MMD government improved allocations in 1993 to some degree but these do not bring expenditure per student back to already inadequate levels of the mid 1980s in either quantitative or qualitative terms. In 1981-85 the education sector took 13.8% of total public expenditure but for 1987-91 the share dropped to 9.8%.

Purely incremental expansion has not been financially viable and a chance to make adult and continuing education, including literacy work, a second major arm of the system which could have reduced educational and social inequalities, was missed in 1978 (Alexander: 1983). The population increased from approximately 5.6 million in 1980 to 7.7 million in 1990 and will be between 10 and 11 million by the year 2,000. 49% of the population are 15 years old or less and about 21% of the population are between 7-13 years which is the primary school age group. The combination of unbalanced population increase and the economic crisis have had the following major effects.

The children of the poor are being squeezed out of the educational system at entry or at latter stages of primary. Up to 1985, primary school enrolment expanded rapidly up to a gross enrolment of 96%. This fell to 88% in 1990, will be lower now and certainly below the population growth rate.

> ... in 1990 approximately 190,000 children of primary school age could find no places in schools. Schools in Lusaka can admit only two thirds of the 7 year old population ...
>
> Ministry of Education (May 1992: iv)

There is over and underage enrolment, double and triple sessions with 50-80 and more in a class to cope with increasing numbers. There are critical shortages of text books, learning materials and any kind of scientific equipment. Teachers morale is low, housing non-existent or in disrepair and salaries insufficient to live on. Salaries account for 97% of the allocation to primary education leaving very little or nothing for learning materials. The quality of education is decreasing and this may result in an increasing lapse back into illiteracy.

> The price that has been paid for the quantitative developments that are so striking is a serious deterioration in the quality of education.
>
> Ibid: 11

The objective of providing a place for all 7 year olds is receding and this has major implications for adult literacy levels. Projected primary enrolment Grade I was 251,200 in 1992 and by 2002 is expected to be 405,480 (Ministry of Education, 1992: 139). In order to keep up with population increase, the need to improve quality, repair dilapidated schools, provide desks, textbooks and equipment and not least to improve teacher morale, real expenditure would have to double over the next ten years. Without massive assistance and the reduction of external debt this is most unlikely. Certainly self-help, community funding and cost-sharing will not be enough given present poverty levels.

The evidence indicates that basic education in Zambia is no longer effective in developing literacy for the young.

> If the present level of illiteracy in the country stands at 49% of the total population of 8 million and there are about 1 million adult illiterates, the calculations indicate that there are over 2 million children and youths who are illiterate.
>
> Lungwangwa (1991: 1)

The small financial allocations to literacy programmes run by the Department of Social Development have not enabled a major impact on adult illiteracy to be made. In 1967 it was possible to enrol 17,000 students but in the other years up to 1986 it was only possible to make approximately 5,000 people literate. Kelly (1991: 62) points out that financial support for the programmes has now dwindled to a nominal sum:

> neglect of this area was underscored by drawing attention to the fact that in almost every one of Zambia's missions abroad education allocations alone receive a larger allocation than the total national commitment to meeting a basic need of almost half the adult population.

There is now an underfunded National Alliance for the Advancement of Literacy which deserves support. The Department of Continuing Education in the Ministry of Education is involved not so much in adult education but with absorbing as many Grade 7 primary school leavers as possible into Open-Secondary programmes with the help of the National Correspondence College. The night-school programme for adults is in decline. There are twelve Schools for Continuing Education providing skills training for out of school youth largely donor funded. The department reached a total of perhaps 25,000 learners each year which in quantitative terms is derisory (Department for Continuing Education, 1992). The department of Youth Development has neither the staff nor the resources to make a significant impact (Office of the President, NCDP, 1994: 116-117). These departments cannot cope with at least 2 million out-of-school youth who are abandoned and live on the abyss of despair.

A recent conference attended by WB, and 'donor' representatives, non-governmental organisations (NGOs) and Zambian representatives has renewed discussion of land tenure in Zambia with a view to opening up even chiefs' land to some form of leasehold or freehold tenure. In another context of trust this might be useful but in terms of the forces of market-place and their agents' analysis, the question is what does Zambia have to offer now? Copper may be exhausted by 2010 but there are other minerals and gem-stones to be exploited. Manufacturing is going out of business due in part to trade 'liberalisation' and unfavourable investment conditions for both Zambian and foreign investors. In terms of human resources the people are sick, undernourished and almost 50% illiterate. One answer is 'the land' and its resources. Already white South African and other farmers are returning. What we are witnessing in Zambia at present is the rape of its economy and the recolonisation of its land, people and resources.

In discussing the purposes of the larger powers, the collapse of the neo-colonial state in Africa, its lack of ability to provide basic social services and at least to act as an honest broker between the people and the larger powers, Paul Wangoola, Secretary of the African Association for Literacy and Adult Education (AALAE) notes two objectives among others:

(vii) Under the cover of 'liberalisation' and 'privatisation' and without a shot, have the peoples of the South surrender to the North, in totality, their resources and assets, and that way turn the peoples of the South into true ' hewers of wood and drawers of water'.

(viii) Impose northern intellectual hegemony, while at the same time choosing a new crop of leaders for the south.

Wangoola (July 1992: 6)

Mbilinyi (1992) in analysing the 'New World Order' from a third world feminist perspective notes the void when it comes to alternative and opposition strategies:

The growth of postmodern and poststructural thought partly reflects this void. However deconstruction methods and the scepticism it nourishes will not by themselves, explain the fundamental causes of crisis or provide viable alternatives. We have to learn how to build as well as to destroy ...

She notes that the crumbling of the cold war makes clear the reality of who controls power and resources. Amidst the despair is a growing critique and the emergence of a new solidarity between men and women of diverse race and national locations in opposition to imperialism in extremely hard times. But the solidarity of understanding between popular movements, new languages of critique and visions of the future require organised forms, the development of alliances and adult educational work if effective action is to occur. Certainly NGOs cannot substitute for independent indigenous social movements with international connections. NGOs, foreign and indigenous, are frequently subverted, co-opted and serve as the grass-roots agents of capital (Mukasa, 1992).

Adult education has historically been associated with progressive social movements concerned with argument, debate and action based on democratic, ethical and moral criteria. Curricula have been concerned with political, economic, philosophical and moral issues related to social justice, equity and mutuality. Liberty and the struggle for it have been and are seen to be grounded in a way of life, in a culture in which individual and civil liberty are mutually embedded and not merely in individual choice. It may well be that the only human rights worth having are not given or legislated for but have to be mutually taken.

The Zambia Congress of Trade Unions (ZCTU), with its affiliated member unions and its educational programmes, is one major social movement which, together with critical feminist, intellectual and professional allies, can form an opposition.

There is not the space here to provide a comprehensive analysis of the Zambian labour movement's development and educational work (see Alexander 1983, 1990 and 1993; Hamalengwa, 1992; Kasase, 1985; Mulenga, 1986; Meebelo, 1971; Rakner, 1992), but the following characteristics are significant.

The labour movement has historically played a crucial role in what were judged to be progressive social, economic and political developments while maintaining its independence from the state and from the political parties it has endorsed. The contribution to the achievement of Independence in 1964 with United National Independence Party (UNIP) and to the electoral success of Movement for Multi-Party Democracy (MMD) in 1991 is clear. The significance of the critical understanding, experience, organisation and political consciousness of Zambian workers and their trade union leadership together with Zambia's deep economic problems and the crisis of legitimacy in UNIP's one-party state combined to produce a massive and relatively peaceful political change and open an era of both hope and danger in the Third Republic. Programmes of workers' education carried out by the ZCTU and affiliated unions have contributed to this critical understanding and consciousness. Since the formal organisation of workers' education in the Department of Education in 1968 workers' educators, with the support of the leadership, resisted all attempts by UNIP to compromise the independence of curriculum in its educational programmes which went together with unsuccessful moves to emasculate and incorporate the labour movement.

It was partly in response to these attempts as well as to UNIP's record of economic failure that in December 1989 the ZCTU Executive Committee approved Chairman General Chiluba's proposal to return to a multi-party political system. Chiluba had since 1974 been Chairman-General of the ZCTU which played a leading role in the development of MMD formed in July 1990 (Mbikusita-Lewanika and Chitala, 1990) and the dismantling of the one-party state established in the second republic in 1972. Chiluba was adopted the Presidential candidate and defeated Kaunda in October 1991. The MMD consisted in 1991 of a broad coalition of trade unionists, businessmen, church-leaders, ex-ministers and ex-members of UNIP united in their opposition to the one-party state, UNIP and the leadership of President Kaunda.

The relationships between knowledge, organisation and power were brought into sharp perspective with trade union leaders expecting that they would be detained if UNIP were returned to office. If the elections had not been won Kaunda and UNIP would have dealt severely with the ZCTU and its continued existence, at least in its present form, would have been threatened. It was recognised that the ZCTU structure, organisation and educational networks w!ere required if MMD was to defeat UNIP. In 1991 the purpose and focus of the ZCTU Department of Education and Training was to educate and involve the labour movement from the top leadership to the rank and file in support of the MMD campaign.

> The year 1991 was a very crucial year for the entire structure of the labour movement during which the Department organised seminars at which the new political thinking was reflected and discussed.
>
> ZCTU (1991: 6)

The ZCTU supported MMD partly on the supposition that the government would act to improve workers' conditions and interests and increase employment, although MMD in their electoral campaign promised an increase in the pace of reforms creating a free market economy which UNIP, under pressure from the WB and IMF, had begun.

Chiluba's position is not entirely clear and he is under intense pressure from WB, IMF and business interests inside and outside the

Cabinet. But he has publicly endorsed the SAP and trade union leaders are now becoming openly critical. There are concerns that the ZCTU and the labour movement may have compromised their traditional independence, assisted the national bourgeoisie to power when it would not have been possible for them to achieve this alone and put firmly in place a rapid shift towards a 'free market' economy, the social effects of which had previously been bitterly condemned by Chiluba.

The labour movement has consistently argued that the free market reforms, removal of subsidies and privatisation of parastatals is going too fast and too far, creating appalling social and human costs including increased unemployment, and that the government has been 'striking while the iron is hot' while it retains sufficient popular support and benefits from the lack of coherent opposition. The view is taken that 'free market' reforms, as shown in Eastern Europe, the countries of the former Soviet Union and Britain, are not the entire answer and that while it is true that authoritarian and bureaucratic communism has failed it is also true that capitalism has not succeeded in the interests of the majority. The position taken in the labour movement is that free market reforms should proceed more carefully and gradually, that the state should retain control of the major public utilities while increasing their efficiency and that Zambia should become a social democracy with a mixed economy. There is concern that land and industry will be taken over by foreign investors together with a small number of Zambians and that the majority of Zambians will not buy shares in a 'property owning democracy' as they patently do not have the resources to do so. It is felt strongly by senior trade union officials that Zambia should deal in its own way with these fundamental issues building on its own history, traditions and culture with particular emphasis on the culture of resistance built up and maintained by the labour movement itself.

After three years of MMD government it is clear that the dominance of the NWO, the conflation of 'democracy, individual human rights', and 'choice' with the 'free market' and the rapid implementation of SAP require the continuing critical presence of a strong independent labour movement as an autonomous social force with control of its own educational programme. Workers' education, the nature of the curriculum and its control, the independence and strength of the Zambian labour movement have formed areas of political conflict and wider cultural struggle which provided important insights into the purposes of UNIP and the state. The content of curriculum in workers' education and the contest for its selection and distribution will continue to provide insights into the purposes of MMD and the state as well as those of the labour movement itself. The nature and quality of the curriculum, its control, purposes and values are the central and concrete issues for adult educators concerned with equity, social justice and democracy.

Despite falling membership and funds due to declining formal employment, the ZCTU has, since early 1991, been developing alternative economic strategies and pressing for more effective tripartite (government, unions and employers) consultation on economic policy, its social effects and the implementation of SAP taking

> cognizance of the fact that since the two contending political parties, namely the MMD and UNIP, had indicated that they would, whichever between them was going to form the next government pursue traditional neo-classical economic policies, at both macro and micro levels, it then became imperative for the trade union movement to appraise itself on these policy reform measures and their implications for workers.
>
> ZCTU (1992: 10)

In its advice to government for the 1994 Budget the ZCTU noted that despite all the measures put in place by government to stabilise the economy there was negative real growth, annual inflation of 200% and massive job losses in the public service, local authorities, parastals and the private sector due to continuing restructuring. The ZCTU urged the government not to continue to rely only on restrictive monetary and fiscal policies to contain the budget deficit and meet debt obligations but to consider other measures to improve investment and employment (ZCTU, December 1993). It is estimated that the ZCTU is going to lose 95,000 of its 350,000 members due to retrenchments and redundancies in the course of implementing SAP. The ZCTU Department of Social and Economic Research together with the Department of Workers' Education is developing educational programmes which assist workers to analyse economic developments which affect their welfare and has, with International Confederation of Free Trade Unions (ICFTU) assistance, embarked on a programme aimed at building capacity in national unions through educating national officers particularly educators, negotiators and researchers (ZCTU, March 1994). The ZCTU Department of Education in its programme for 1994 noted that the main threat to democracy is widespread poverty:

The most important challenge in our era is finding ways and means to enable workers to survive the realities of the SAP which has brought untold misery and poverty on peasants and workers in Zambia. Changes taking place in the political, social and economic life of the country need to be carefully studied and thoroughly understood by workers and union leaders so that we manoeuvre through the situation in a much more rational and positive way if our newly founded democracy is to be safeguarded. To this effect workers' education is going to play an important role in consolidating Democracy.

ZCTU (1993: 2)

Mr Shamenda, Chairman General of ZCTU remarked in August 1994 during a speech to the European Union/African, Carribean, Pacific trade union conference on Lome IV in Lusaka that free trade unions are fighting for their survival, that it is not possible to speak about human rights without addressing trade union and workers' rights and that:

Trade unions must build their capacity to offer alternative policies and enable social partners to effectively participate in the development of programmes for growth and employment.

There is a clear recognition on the part of trade unionists and workers' educators of the danger of an incorporation of the independent Zambian labour movement and its educational programme into the neo-liberal project. There is also concern in the labour movement that the hidden agenda of Zambia's business groupings together with their international allies is to encourage disunity in the trade unions and the formation of more than one national centre for the labour movement thus destroying its strength, autonomy and solidarity (Alexander, 1993). A senior Zambian trade union official arguing vehemently for the continued strength and importance of a unified and independent labour movement in a political climate unsympathetic to trade unions commented in August 1992:

Workers educators must go towards the goal of understanding the 'New World Order' in order to deal with it and challenge it locally.

The strength of a culture of resistance and hope based on Zambian history, knowledge, experience and action is about to be tested to the full.

Note

Anthropometry

The measurement of weights and heights of children aged between 3 and 59 months allowed the calculation of indicators of malnutrition namely, stunting, wasting and under-nutrition. The results indicate that malnutrition is widespread in Zambia with 39, 22 and 6 percent of children being stunted, under-nourished and wasted respectively.

The rural areas exhibit higher incidences of stunting and under-nourished than the urban areas of 46 and 25 percent as compared to 35 and 20 percent respectively. Male children are more likely to be malnourished than their female counterparts. It is estimated that 41, 24 and 8 percent of male children as compared to 36, 19 and 5 percent of their female counterparts are stunted, under-nourished and wasted respectively.

The incidences of stunting and under-nutrition are highest at age group 13 to 18 months and are both lowest at age 3 to 6 months, while that of wasting is highest at age group 19 to 24. Children of highly educated mothers have lower incidences of malnutrition in general. Female headed households have higher incidence of malnutrition among their children than those male headed.

Central Statistical Office (1993)

References

Adedeji, A. (ed.) (1993). *Africa within the World: Beyond Dispossession and Dependence.* African Centre for Development and Strategic Studies.

Adepoju, J. (ed.) (1993). *The Impact of Structural Adjustment on the Population of Africa: The Implications for Education, Health and Employment.* James Currey.

Alexander, D.J. (1983). Problems of educational reform in Zambia. *International Journal of Education Development*, Vol 3, No 2, 203-222.

Alexander, D.J. (1990). The Politics of Workers' Education in Zambia. *International Journal of Lifelong Education*, Vol 9 No 3, 179-200.

Alexander, D.J. (1993). *The Development of Workers' Education and Political Change in Zambia.* Occasional Paper No 42, Centre of African Studies, Edinburgh University.

Alexander, D.J. and Martin, I. (1995). Competence, curriculum and democracy. In *Adult Education: Critical Intelligence and Social Change* (eds. J. Thompson and M. Mayo). Leicester: NIACE.

Central Statistical Office, Republic of Zambia (1993). *Social Dimensions of Adjustment: Priority Survey I 1991 Report*. Lusaka.

Chirwa, A. (August 1994). *Opening Remarks to Skills Training Seminar for Women Organisers: Kapiri Mposhi*. (Mimeo) Kitwe: ZCTU.

Cornia, G.A., Van Der Hoeven, R. and Mkandawire, T. (eds.) (1992). *Africa's Recovery in the 1990s: From Stagnation and Adjustment to Human Development*._UNICEF.

Department of Continuing Education (1992). *Annual Report for the year 1991*. Lusaka: Ministry of Education.

Fasheh, M. (1992). West Bank: learning to survive. In *Community Education in the Third World* (eds. C. Poster and J.C. Zimmer), pp. 17-29. Routledge.

Giddens, A. (1994) What's Left for Labour. *New Statesman and Society*. 30th September 1994, 37-40.

Graham-Brown, S. (1991). *Education in the Developing World: Conflict and Crisis*. Longman.

Griffin, C. (1983). *Curriculum Theory in Adult and Lifelong Education*. Croom Helm.

Hamalengwa, M. (1992). *Class Struggles in Zambia 1889-1989 and The Fall of Kenneth Kaunda 1990-91*. University Press of America.

Hobsbawm, E. (1994). *The Age of Extremes — The Short 20th Century, 1914-1991*. Michael Joseph.

Inglis, F. (1988). *Popular Culture and Political Power*. Harvester/Wheatsheaf.

International Confederation of Free Trade Unions (ICFTU), Zambia Congress of Trade Unions (ZCTU), and Fredrich Ebert Stiftung (FES) (1992). *The Social Dimensions of Adjustment in Zambia*. Lusaka.

International Labour Organisation (January 1994). *Report of the Director General*. Eighth African Regional Conference, Mauritius. Geneva: I.L.O.

Kalyalya, D.H. and Muuka, G.N. (1994). *Structural Adjustment, Macroeconomic Demand Management, Food Policy Reform and its impact on Rural and Urban Poverty in Zambia*. Paper presented to Malawi Seminar on Integration of Poverty Alleviation Strategies into Economic Policies, ll-20 July 1994.

Kapijimpanga, O. (1994). *Towards a Zambian Coalition on Debt and Development*. Paper presented to the Economics Association of Zambia, August 5th-6th 1994, Lusaka.

Kasase, W.K. (1985). Workers' Education for Industrial Democracy: The Zambian Experience 1978-83. Unpublished M.A. dissertation. The Hague, Institute of Social Studies.

Keddie, N. (1980). Adult education: an ideology of individualism. In *Adult Education for a Change* (ed. J. Thompson), pp. 45-64. Hutchinson.

Kelly, M.J. (March 1991). *The Funding and Costing of Basic Education for All.* Lusaka: Mulungushi Hall.

King, B. (1991). Comments on Mohsen A. Fardi's paper on 'Zambia: Reform and Reversal' in *Restructuring Economies in Distress* (eds. V. Thomas et al.). Washington D.C.: World Bank.

Lungwangwa, G. (March 1991). *Policies and Strategies to Improve the Quality of Basic Education in Zambia.* National Conference on Education for All, Mulungushi Hall, Lusaka.

Mbikusita-Lewanika, A. and Chitala, D. (eds.) (1990). *The Hour has Come! Proceedings of the National Conference on the Multi-Party Option.* Lusaka: Zambia Research Foundation.

Mbilinyi, M. (July 1992). An Overview of Issues in the Political Economy of Adult Education in the 1990s. Conference paper, International workshop on the *Political Economy of Adult Education in the 1990s and Beyond: Theoretical and Practical Challenges,* Mombasa, Kenya. African Association of Literacy and Adult Education (AALAE).

Meebelo, H.S. (1971). *Reaction to Colonialism: A Prelude to the Politics of Independence in Northern Rhodesia 1893-1939.* Manchester University Press.

Ministry of Education (May 1992). *Focus on Learning.* Lusaka.

Mukasa, E.H. (July 1992). The Nature of Imperialism in the 1990s and the Implications for Adult Education. Conference paper, International workshop on the *Political Economy of Adult Education in the 1990s and Beyond: Theoretical and Practical Challenges,* Mombasa, Kenya. AALAE.

Mulenga, P.A. (1986). An Evaluation of Workers' Education in Zambia. Unpublished Diploma dissertation. University of Zambia, Lusaka.

Muuka, G.N. (1993). The Impact of Zambia's 1983-1993 Structural Adjustment Programme on Business Strategy. Unpublished PhD thesis. University of Edinburgh.

Office of the President, National Commission for Development Planning (1992). *Public Investment Programme 1992-95.* Lusaka.

Office of the President, Planning Division (1992). *Economic Review (January-March 1992)*. Lusaka.

Office of the President, NCDP (January 1994). *Economic Report 1993*. Lusaka.

Rakner, L. (1992). *Trade Unions in Processes of Democratisation: A Study of Party/Labour Relations in Zambia*. Chr. Michelsen Institute, Department of Social Science and Development, Norway.

Rau, B. (1991). *From Feast to Famine*. ZED Books.

Republic of Zambia (1990). *Social Action Programme 1990-93*. Government Printer, Lusaka.

Seshemani, V. (1992). The Economic Policies of Zambia in the 1980s: Towards Structural Transformation with a Human Focus. In *Africa's Recovery in the 1990s* (eds. G.A. Cornia et al.) pp. 116-134. UNICEF.

Torres, A.C. (April 1991). A critical review of the education for all background documents. In *Perspectives on Education for All*, International Development Research Centre (Canada), pp. 1-20.

United Nations Development Programme (1990). *Human Development Report 1990*. New York.

Wangoola, P. (July 1992). Alternative Forms of Organisation and Social Action: Implications for Adult and Community Education. Conference paper, International workshop on the *Political Economy of Adult Education in the 1990s and Beyond: Theoretical and Practical Challenges*, Mombasa, Kenya. AALAE.

World Conference on Education for All (September 1989). *Meeting Basic Learning Needs: A New Vision for the 1990s*. Background Document. Jomtien, Thailand, 5-9 March 1990.

World Conference on Education for All (1990). *World Declaration on Education for All: Framework for Action to Meet Basic Learning Needs*. Jomtien, Thailand, UNDP, UNESCO, UNICEF, World Bank.

Zambia Congress of Trade Unions (1991). *Report of the Secretary General for the year 1991*. (Mimeo) ZCTU, Kitwe.

Zambia Congress of Trade Unions (1992). *Programmes and Budget for 1992*. (Mimeo) ZCTU, Kitwe.

Zambia Congress of Trade Unions (December 1993). *Proposed Areas of Focus for the MMD Government Budget for 1994*. (Mimeo) ZCTU, Kitwe.

Zambia Congress of Trade Unions (1993). *Workers' Education and Training Programme: January to December 1994.* (Mimeo) ZCTU, Kitwe.

Zambia Congress of Trade Unions (March 1994). *Department of Social and Economic Research: Annual Report for 1993 and Work Plan for 1994.* (Mimeo) ZCTU, Kitwe.

Adult Education, the 'Critical' Citizen and Social Change

John Wallis and Paula Allman

> ... I find it difficult to stomach this casual rejection of the [liberal] tradition which nourished us, this uncritical acceptance of the values of our time, and I cannot get rid of the conviction that our society and our universities still need an adult education movement which challenges and questions [values and] assumptions.
>
> Wiltshire (1956: 36)

Many times Harold Wiltshire expressed himself in a way that demonstrated his profound commitment to the 'social good'. He was a person with a 'social consciousness' who did not dichotomise the betterment of the social from the development of the individual. In fact, he seems to have realised that individual fulfilment could come only from an active engagement in shaping the direction of development of one's community and nation. In other words, he had a firm view on the meaning of democracy and its relationship to the full development of individuals through the praxis of citizenship.

In this article, we may agree in principle with the thrust of his ideas; however we will have to debate the substance — the actual 'acceptability' he seems to have attributed to the concepts of democracy, and therefore citizenship. Like so many liberals and progressives and even contemporary radicals, Wiltshire thought a social movement, in his case the adult education movement, could work with the 'grain of the times', by infusing social changes with well tested traditional values and objectives. He did not want to directly challenge the present and future but to be sure they were influenced by the very best of what had been developed educationally in the past. He referred to this, in the article cited above, as the 'Great Tradition'; we know it better as the liberal tradition of adult education.

In passing it is perhaps of value to consider the relationship of recent analytical trends to the liberal tradition. The reference to specific historical circumstances or 'times' came to particular prominence at the end of the 1980s when social analysts — especially those associated with the journal *Marxism Today* — concluded that a new social order had come into being, which they generally referred to as 'new Times' (see Hall and Jacques, 1989). The gist of their analysis of the new regime of capital implied that the new forms of accumulation — transnational, at the same time small-scale and fragmented, yet centralised via the new electronic media of communication, and generating new demands for 'flexible' forms of labour — demanded new approaches to the issue of human oppression in its multiple forms. Under such circumstances the 'old' ways of thinking were no longer appropriate: they had arisen under different circumstances of 'modernity' with its emphasis on mass production, the masculine proletariat and a faith in the enlightenment project of reason. These old ways of understanding now ran against the grain of the new order, and new visions of future development were required that would acknowledge the difference existing within and between groups which had previously been treated as homogeneous categories e.g. 'black' people, women, class. At the same time that difference was to be celebrated — even at the level of the individual — ways were to be sought to combine groups together to form a progressive force at the level of the social order in general.

The rather parodic account above is included to underline the extent to which the established liberal beliefs have recently been under attack in a renewed form. The onslaught has not been on the essentially bourgeois nature of liberal rationalism, nor the limitations of its epistemology, but on the very relevance of the project itself. If we are at the end of the enlightenment project, and if the 'grand narratives' associated with it are dead, then the struggle to develop the citizen as we have thus far understood the term for either left or right is simply irrelevant.

Such analysis, with its resonance of post-structural and postmodern thought, has not been uncontested (see Jameson, 1991; Harvey, 1989), but is a reference to highlight the intellectual terrain on which the liberal tradition has had to move in recent years. Liberal educators such as Wiltshire did not seek to challenge the basic liberal democratic order, but sought to influence its trajectory in a 'humanising' direction. Such educators derive from the tradition going back to Matthew Arnold whose faith in the moral effects of education often form a sub-text in liberal writing. It is a tradition that has produced heroes for both left and right, and it should be noted that there can be more than a strain of elitism in this stance, clearly evidenced in writers such as Eliot and Leavis (see Milner, 1994), but equally apparent at times in the work of Wiltshire himself.

Thus, although the liberal tradition maintains the right of *all* people to have access to the best of what has been thought and said, it is accepted from the outset that not all people will be able to use the opportunity. It is assumed that although all people are equal some will inevitably be more capable of reflection than others.

In the 1980s and 1990s many adult educators have been shocked by how easily the values of the liberal tradition have disappeared from the discourses and agendas of vast areas of adult education. Just as we must ask why Wiltshire's challenge in the seemingly propitious 1950s had so little long-term effect, we must examine why the values of that tradition are seemingly so ineffectual in the current educational climate. This is not to say that adult educators have accepted the erosion of their service without resistance. There has been a spirited defence against the crude 'vocationalism' that has been imposed on adult education work, with its spuriously defined and restricting forms (see Hyland, 1994), and the philosophical principles of the new right have been effectively criticised by established liberal educators (see Lawson in this volume). However, the values that would have generated a broad defence seem to be ill-rooted in the wider society.

We will argue that part of the problem lies, and has always been located, in a 'leap of faith' which was demanded from those who were the proponents and supporters of the liberal tradition. As mentioned above, this 'leap' relates to the connection between engagement in liberal education and its moral effects. In some unspecified way access to the 'humanities' develops within the individual not only increased cognitive skill and understanding, but also a sense of civic responsibility that once applied will inevitably lead to broad social improvement. It is this discourse which gives the liberal tradition both its social importance and its claim to be a movement based on unimpeachable moral grounds.

However, it may be difficult to question these connections without first questioning the assumed meaning of the fundamental terms — education, citizen and democracy. This is what we intend to do. In so doing we hope to indicate our broad agreement with a concept of progress and respect for many of the values and objectives of the liberal tradition, but also to pose alternative concepts of those fundamental terms which could revitalise the adult education movement so that it could begin to effectively challenge the current trends in adult education in 'Our Times'. Perhaps it goes without saying, but we will need to argue for a much more radical perspective of social purpose and social change.

Firstly, we need to locate our argument within what has been termed an alternative radical tradition in adult education (see e.g. Thomas and Westwood, 1991; Thomas, 1982). Initially, this tradition can best be grasped by seeing a distinction between struggles over many years to gain access for excluded groups to established forms of education, and attempts to locate control of education — including the curriculum — in the hands of the excluded — whether defined by race, gender, class, etc. In the first case, radicalism has often been seen in terms of innovation in form — ranging from the paternalism of the old universities in establishing extra-mural provision in the 19th century to the much more evanescent outreach projects of recent years. The key to this kind of radical work is that in all cases the efforts are addressed at 'enabling' access to the established disciplines via provision suited to the target (usually excluded or pathologised) audience. This form of radicalism is closely allied to the liberal tradition in that the aims of the endeavours are the same: everyone has the right to have contact with our established culture. However, what will be ultimately learned and the forms in which such knowledge will be appropriated remain largely unquestioned. Our current concern with access courses into higher education and their myriad forms is perhaps a current manifestation of this element. If such work is successful, the 'silent' will find their voice in a liberal pluralist democracy.

Set against this access tradition is an approach to the education of adults that acknowledges that what is learned itself carries a dimension of power, and control over curriculum content is of central concern. Historically, this is best seen in the distinction between the 'neutral' knowledge propagated by the establishment and 'really useful knowledge' aimed at revealing the inherently oppressive nature of the current social order, and equipping participants to engage in a struggle to change the status quo (see Johnson, 1979). In this tradition, we find debates concerning whether a liberatory education can be provided by a capitalist state, and above all, the demand that what is learnt, the curriculum, should remain in the hands of the oppressed groups. The important issue was/is to learn how to change an oppressive reality, and the value of knowledge can be judged by the degree to which it contributes to that end. Here we have moved our concept of empowerment away from finding an active place in liberal democracy to a more directly oppositional form of social intervention, and the clear rejection of the liberal concept of the 'neutrality' of knowledge.

These latter initiatives have more in common with our own concept of what the radical tradition is about. Workers in the past, perhaps, went as far as they could in their times, but we think the possibility for going much further is available now, available to all radical educators as well as many of our liberal colleagues. However, the liberatory strategy will only be effective, i.e. realised in the educational experience of adults, if we can collaborate to achieve our common principles and engage in a very serious and open debate on the meaning of those principles and the means by which we enable people to experience them. As mentioned earlier the challenge of finding a means to authentically unify those groups who have either a material or ethical interest in ending oppression is a major concern.

We would reject the naive assumption that groups can join together automatically around some area of common interest over a sustained period unless, of course, they have themselves engaged in considerable educational/cultural work to come to a clear understanding of their specific historical context. Such a stance would challenge some of the more naive assumptions made about the potential common interests of disparate groupings, associated with the 'new movements' debates of the 1980s (e.g. Ekins, 1992). To reach such a situation would require considerable 'pre-figurative' work. We would sympathise with Gramsci's view that current — often incoherent — aspirations to change must be developed into a major social force:

> A historic act can only be performed by 'collective man', and this pre-supposes the attainment of a 'cultural-social' unity through which a multiplicity of dispersed wills, with heterogeneous aims, are welded together with a single aim, on the basis of an equal and common conception of the world, both general and particular ... where the intellectual base is so well-rooted, assimilated and experienced that it becomes a passion.
>
> Gramsci (1971: 349)

In this context the concept of democratic action is fundamentally re-defined.

To make explicit what we have only implied — we agree that there must be a link, a direct connection, between education (particularly adult education) — citizenship — democracy -the social good, and that these are also directly related to social change. These must be the social purpose of that adult education movement. However, by analysing the substance, the meaning of these principles, we intend to show that real connections can be realised in the practice and theory of adult education. Since everything we will propose hinges on the concept of democracy, we will begin with that.

Rebuilding and re-creating democracy

One cannot escape the irony that the very historical moment when democracy has been proclaimed and heralded as the only possible destiny for humankind (see Fukuyama, 1992) coincides with a most pervasive apathy amongst the citizens of the current forms of democratic society. And yet, it is not ironical if we consider the form of democracy that has been *granted* in response to peoples' struggles throughout history to create and shape the societies in which they live — to be the legitimate subject or agents of their historical destinies not just the objects of a dominant class's attempts to maintain 'their' social order. This 'granted' democracy has never been anything but the appearance of a compromise between the aspirations of the vast majority of people and the needs of those whose interests are inextricably interwoven with the preservation of the capitalist social form. We need to look directly at the nature of that compromise — the nature of what can best be termed liberal democracy.

As Hall (1982) clearly pointed out, the now familiar form of Western democracy involved the 'wedding' of two quite different philosophies and value systems. One addressed the economics of the social order; the other focused on the political and social realms of that order. Bringing the two together involved considerable compromise. Liberal ideas focused on individuals acting in their own 'rational' self-interest within rules of 'fairness', whereby the equality of market exchanges would promote the 'social good'. Government, the state, was to play a minimal role, somewhat like an amenable referee who, while observing the basic rules, does not block the progress of the game. In this competitive game scenario, the competition was for the economic prosperity of the individual winner. Also, it was assumed that the success of any particular individual would mean that the losers would reap some advantage from the achievements of the talented: they would benefit indirectly as the individual's success would contribute to the economic well-being of the wider society. This economic logic has been seen recently in the claims that the espousal of 'free' market principles guarantees benefits for all via a 'trickle down' effect: hence, to inhibit the economically skilful may damage all.

On the other hand, the original philosophy of democracy was grounded on the assumption that people needed to work together to shape their collective and individual destinies. Government was to be a government of the people, by the people and for the people; and this was supposed to mean 'all the people' not some socio-economic class, cadre of political experts or intellectual elite.

Both philosophies had merit in theory but seem never in history to have escaped the damaging effects brought out by their grounding in reality. Perhaps it was their mutual limitations that made their seeming disparateness reconcilable in the final compromise that produced the forms of liberal democracies that we have experienced. We will focus on only a few of the fundamental difficulties.

Firstly, as far as liberal theory goes, it was/is well nigh impossible to get individuals to play the game by the rules which the principles dictate. Even Adam Smith warned of this but probably never fully conceived how a much stronger bourgeois state would have to evolve to regulate social economic exchange and guarantee what we now call negative freedoms and liberties (see Held, 1987). Furthermore, the whole 'liberal' concept of equality, originally the exchange of equivalents, was entirely undermined when human labour power itself became the only life sustaining commodity most people could exchange within the social relations of capitalism. As Marx pointed out, within capitalist economies, the labour commodity can never be exchanged for an equivalent, a wage equivalent to the labour time expended, as this relation of inequality or non-equivalence is the fundamental basis of the capitalist social form and the source of surplus value, the source of capitalist profit.

Also, democratic theory was compromised from its inception in, as far as we know, ancient Athens. However, the difficulties in this context are not so deep rooted in the sense that they relate to the practical application of the process rather than to the basic principles. We will highlight only one of the substantive concepts but one which reveals a great deal about how our own history of struggle for democracy resulted in the 'liberal' compromise. The Athenians are celebrated for their practice of 'direct' democracy wherein 'all the people', i.e. all citizens, rather than only their representatives, had a voice in governing the city state. However, as is now very well known, their concept of citizen was one which excluded the vast majority of people engaged in socially and domestically productive work, viz all slaves and free women. Ever since, democracy usually has only been introduced as a governing form when it rides on the back of an exclusive concept of the citizen. In our history property ownership, literacy and gender have been used as the arguments for exclusion. This exclusivity has meant at least two things. Firstly, liberal philosophy could accommodate the principles and values of democracy in an abstract or formal sense, while leaving certain areas of social life undemocratised and certain groups excluded. In this sense, the 'wedding' of apparently conflicting values was patriarchal in form, with the values of democracy compromising far more than was necessary for the liberal partner. Secondly, at the practical level, it also meant that the vast majority of historical struggles for democracy have been over access to the evolving, given, compromised form of democracy. They have involved arduous and dangerous struggles by excluded groups to gain access to the vote and the other rights of citizens. They have also more recently involved struggles to spread democracy to various areas of civil society and the economy. Rarely have these struggles contested the form and nature of democracy, so well developed in political life, which currently engenders reactions ranging from apathy to outright disgust amongst the electorates of Western democratic states.

If democracy is the progressive and promised destiny for humankind, it is urgent that we begin to debate its meaning and the meaning of the concepts which provide the practice of democracy with an authentic substance. It is urgent because if we don't rebuild democracy by reshaping it into a liberatory form, more and more people in the world will experience the result of their struggles as a sham and quite possibly eschew democratic principles in favour of some form of authoritarian certainty. The debate is especially urgent because we have only to open our eyes and ears to see that liberal-democracy has little or highly questioned meaning to citizens, East or West, who are experiencing the crisis in the capitalist global economy (see Mishler and Rose, 1993). However, the debate will have to involve far more than the meaning of democracy and its substantive concepts. If we decide to rebuild democracy by re-creating it, we will need to give serious deliberation to the necessary preparations, in particular the preparation of people who will be capable of shaping their own social, political, economic and environmental destiny, and this requires that the adult education movement, as well as education in general, must play a central role in both the debates and the preparation. What we will propose is an agenda for how adult education might take a proactive role in shaping the future of social change via the promotion of critically intelligent and active citizens. However, first we must outline our own vision of a re-created democracy. We hasten to add that this is not a blue print but simply some considered suggestions that might stimulate the necessary debate.

Our vision is based on a current analysis of our material reality, i.e. what is at hand and therefore possible to realise at this point in historical development. In other words the technology is available, although perhaps not used in the way we will advocate, and the values are present, although submerged because they are not elevated and promoted at a societal level. Also, it appears that we have the ability to produce sufficient products and services to meet human need, as well as the values and experiences which could redirect such production according to the satisfaction of human need rather than the denial of that in favour of the competitive creation of capitalist profit. The first re-creation we want to propose has to do with time.

We remember that once, in a seminar, Wiltshire talked about the necessity of re-creating our division of time. He felt every citizen should divide their time between activities devoted to work, leisure and social purpose. We totally agreed; however his was a concept of the individual voluntary allocation of time and ours involves a vision of a social structure which would actively promote such a commitment, together with a greater integration of the divided social activities referred to. In this sense, re-creating our use of time is essential to re-creating democracy. Some experiments in democracy have viewed the devotion of time to governing as a right and responsibility of all citizens to take on in turn, and it is perhaps ironic that systems as different as the Paris Commune and the United States House of Representatives should share this principle. In other words there could be some time during a week, or a short period of the citizen's life, where one is expected, and remunerated like any other productive worker, to engage in active political and social participation in one's community and the wider national society.

This feature of the debate has a direct relevance to current social circumstances when some influential politicians are attempting to put the issue of employment at the top of the political agenda and when so many millions of people are desperate for them to do so. Of course, many people would argue that full employment defined in any sense is impossible to achieve because of the need to be at the cutting edge of technological advance, which often means fewer jobs. This social feature has long been seen as an essential characteristic of the climate of intensified global competition (see Thrift, 1986). However, their argument assumes capitalist social relations of production and production for profit rather than production directed at meeting human needs outside market relations. We wish to argue that we could perceive and realise our goals differently; but we could also use technology within different social relations to allow each of us enough time away from producing useful products for human consumption to actively engage in producing the broad social order in which we experience and may even come en masse to enjoy our existence. Some very critical and creative thinking about time is essential, and this must include not only 'working' time calculated as percentages of weeks or months, but also the way in which we interweave the time we allocate to our rights and responsibilities within our life-plans. One doesn't have to make a great leap in imagination to consider the beneficial effects such re-creative uses of time could have on our future ageing populations, to say nothing of the present and future benefits for the rest of us destined to join that currently oppressed group. It is impossible, however, to believe that any such structural time re-creation could even be contemplated without a great deal of dialogue aimed at fostering a consensus for change. The social creation of such change would be dependent on the values upon which these changes would be predicated: in other words those values which promote the realisation of our full human potential.

Having suggested the above it seems to us obvious that our concept of education must be similarly re-created if we are to enable any re-creation of our democracies. Later in this article we will devote considerable space to offering alternative ideas about the social relations of education and the form of dialogue which is a consequence of them. However, at this point we need to mention the content of education. If people are going to collectively transform their democracies through, in the first and fundamental instance, restructuring their use of time, they will need to know what is possible, including: technological capabilities and possibilities; alternative ideas about democracy and citizenship and alternative forms of education which could prepare us to create and participate fully in a national and global society.

Before moving on to education, we must suggest or reiterate a few more re-creations that are essential to the rebuilding of democracy. Most of these seem to depend upon a re-creative use of time which could be substantially developed — even under capitalist social relations — if these were to be regulated by the politics of social democracy. However, the full realisation of some of these suggestions may well be impossible in the absence of more fundamental social change and transformation. Nevertheless, we can begin, even now, the struggles to place them on, and then move them to the top of, the political agenda.

Academic or theoretical debates around the form of democracy tend to take an either/or direction. In some circles the debate is caught within the framework of representative democracy and tends to focus on questions regarding the nature of the actual representatives. Should they be selected from the total range of citizens or should they be selected from those educated and cultured in a manner which has 'prepared' them for leadership or even those born to lead? In radical circles the arguments for forms of more direct democracy have been kept alive. We would suggest that the form, at whatever level of civic life, must be rationally and democratically chosen on the basis of whether the form is consistent with achieving the best form of governance at that level. Therefore we could create democratic structures which interweave a variety of forms at all levels and even forms which are dynamic and, as a consequence, are responsive to historically specific circumstances. This would require citizen flexibility or the willingness to participate to a limited degree all the time but to a greater degree at specific times. Here we move on to a suggestion that has to do with additional change, but to reiterate, one which would have to be facilitated by the re-creation of time.

In recent years in the UK, the idea of 'rights' has been at the forefront of political discourse. However, rights have been largely de-coupled from the idea of responsibility. In democracies equal emphasis must be put on both, but to correct the current imbalance in emphasis, we also may need to stress the rights, as well as the responsibilities, of citizens as a collective body rather than solely as individuals — which is the present emphasis. If we do not, then responsibility will be individualised and any individual 'shortcomings' will be pathologised when absent. In this sense a democratic form will be reactive rather than proactive, as we visualise it must be for the future of democracy.

Our last suggestion is a reiteration in more explicit form of something we said earlier. A great deal of twentieth century theorising about democracy has assumed that more direct forms of democracy and citizen participation are impossible in complex societies. Had we not developed the technology of telecommunications, albeit for different purposes, this stance might be difficult to refute. But in fact this is refutable because the technology exists, and the abilities to adapt it also exist. Current possibilities would allow democratic citizens to communicate at long, even global, distances: to inform, debate, compromise and creatively engage in decision making. Those who control our economic world are already linked in this way. There is no reason why we cannot utilise these achievements of human development to re-create democracy — to use them not only to interlink our political thinking but to integrate, or explicitly re-integrate, the political with the economic realms of our decision making and popular democratic control. Of course, we must have the will, rather than only the ability to do this, and the creation of such a will amongst the mass of the citizens of our world may depend on social transformations wherein these ideas could be actively promoted and supported. For the present, this is where rebuilding the adult education movement becomes of great importance. Authentic will, an authentic change in values will not be achieved by social engineering, although social structures can support such change. Adult education, in our times, might once again become a movement for the social good if we prioritise placing a critique of the present and a serious consideration of the real possibilities for humanity's future at the top of our curricular agenda. In the next section we will argue that to do this we need to enable people to experience education within alternative social relations that would offer them both the knowledge of and an experience of the possibilities for a better, more just, more authentically democratic future.

Re-creating an adult education that could contribute to rebuilding democracy:

In the first instance we must move our objectives from enabling the development of the reflective citizen to the objective of developing critical citizens. There is a simple, but fundamental difference. The reflective citizen reflects, often critically, on how well the present state of affairs is developing, or whether our liberal-democracy and capitalist economy are working to promote prosperity and the maintenance of the social order. Critical citizens question the present state of affairs and also its history, the assumptions and special interests that have led to its development. They assess contemporary circumstances in terms of an ontological position which is critical of the present because of a vision of more fully developed human beings. In other words, this is a critique of how the present frameworks limit what we are, judged in accord with materially derived criteria pertaining to what we could become. Critical citizens not only challenge the present but propose, and wherever possible, implement, alternative, more just and humane social relations whilst continually assessing whether these enable us to move towards a fuller realisation of our human potential. This critical approach to reality is needed at every level of human activity be it political, social or economic.

As educators there is a great deal we can do to set the process of preparation for an authentic democracy into action. In the following we will describe how we have developed the process in the area of adult education, or more precisely the professional development of those who work educationally with adults.

In our practice we would find it impossible to separate the discussion of process from that of content as is frequently done in adult education. This is because we are intent upon offering the experience of transformed and very different social relations, including the learning groups' relation to knowledge. This concern with the relation to knowledge involves the way in which learners and teachers relate to academic knowledge, but also addresses the knowledge base that informs values and beliefs, and areas of 'common sense' which are constitutive of a person's identity. In other words, we do not think that actual persons can effect a transformation in the way they relate to one another without simultaneously trying to relate to what they, and others, think or know in a very revolutionary way.

Many adult educators believe in and try to achieve a non-hierarchical or more harmonious relationship between teachers and learners. The discourses of adult education are full of 'politically correct' terms, such as, 'student centred', 'unconditional positive regard', 'relevance' and 'starting where the learner is'. We have worked within the regimes of these discourses and found them wanting when judged by both authenticity and the achievement, for all, of creative and critical thought. Therefore, after considerable experience, we turned towards, and have worked arduously in our own practice to implement, the educational philosophy of the Brazilian educationalist, Paulo Freire. Freire (1972) insists upon simultaneous ontological and epistemological transformations — we cannot be together and learn together differently without coming to know in a very different way, which enables us to create 'new knowledge' or a much deeper, clearer and critically assessed way of knowing or understanding what we already know.

Of course, attempting to transform simultaneously both epistemological and ontological relations complicates the process of creating an alternative experience of education. On their own, and through force of personality, educators can create less hierarchical social relations amongst students and themselves; however, what we advocate and practise holds the promise of going much deeper in terms of penetrating the very essence of our social being. But it involves a collective and co-operative, and always explicit, struggle to transform the way we relate to knowledge and thought. Therefore, it is not in the gift of the educator to work as the exclusive transformer of relations. The educator must challenge existing practice, initiate a new process, support the learners, exemplify the principles in all he or she does and challenge again with support as often as necessary. Nevertheless, in the end, these transformations can only result from a collectively committed effort. The general direction of the transformed student-teacher relation seems to be generally appreciated amongst adult educators. We will return to it later after elaborating on the transformed epistemological relations or relations to knowledge.

Freire (especially 1972) explains the epistemological transformation in his writings; therefore it is surprising that so many enthusiasts for and critics of his philosophy ignore this fundamental element. In addition to his writings we have been fortunate to have access to a series of audio tapes recorded by the Australian Council of Churches during Freire's visit to Australia in 1974. In one of these he explains the transformation through a critique of current epistemologies. For clarity, we slightly paraphrase what he says:

'Let me be clear. The teachers I criticise often work very hard and very seriously. They go to their studies, or the library, and research the topic which will constitute the lesson for their next class and they prepare that lesson thoroughly. However, once the lesson is prepared, their 'act of knowing' is complete, is finished. I am convinced of just the opposite. To know, to know more deeply, I need another 'subject' (person) of knowing. The knowledge must be a medium which evokes the critical reflection of both the teacher and the students, together they are critical co-investigators in dialogue'.

It is clear to us that this reference to established teaching practice is a critique of a particular epistemology not a critique of method because it can pertain equally to traditional and progressive pedagogies. It is also clear from everything that Freire says and writes that both the ontological and epistemological transformations must be promoted through engaging in the unique form of human communication he calls dialogue.

Dialogue is central to Freire's concept of problem-posing education. In dialogue we are required to not just share what we know, as we might in a discussion, but to ask ourselves and others why we think as we do, where our thinking has come from in terms of both personal and societal history and whose interests it serves. We are also required to pose these questions with reference to 'cognizable objects', the focal 'content' which mediates the participants in dialogue. The 'cognizable objects' might be books, journal articles or videos which promote an explanation of some phenomenon the group is co-investigating.

The phenomena which constitute the curriculum relate directly to what Freire calls 'generative themes'. Such themes enable learners to come to a critical reading of the world — to understand what is happening and why it is happening as well as what would be necessary to change it. This is the type of understanding which would be required of critical citizens. These themes not only depict the world as a totality but relate to or generate into one another; they link to one another and manifest themselves at all levels of human existence, i.e. locally and globally (see Freire 1972, Chapter 2-3).

It is important to emphasise that people engaged in this form of education are not only developing critical understanding. They come to this understanding within dialogue; therefore they are also experiencing and learning a way of communicating which seems to us extremely appropriate for all types of democratic participation. Because dialogue is the 'seal' of the transformed epistemological and ontological relations, it develops both critical thought and trusting, harmonious relations between those who engage in it. In educational contexts, this means authentically transformed student/teacher relations.

Freire's educational approach was designed to prepare us to achieve our ontological vocation, a calling to strive to become more fully human. For those of us who believe in the principle of democracy, who see it as the best possible means for organising our social existence in a way that enables us to respond to our vocation, it comes as no surprise that Freire's approach is directly linked to the ideals of democracy and the development of critical citizens. Once his philosophy is understood, no leap of faith is required to apprehend the direct connection between Freirean education, effective citizen and the democratisation of human activity. However, even with this form of education, there is still one leap of faith required.

People who engage in Freirean education must have a profound faith in human beings. This involves believing in the potential of all people to develop the creative and critical abilities required for humanising the world. It also involves the belief that once people 'read their world' critically, they will have the desire to engage in the necessary transformations. Freire (1972) expresses clearly what this faith entails.

Dialogue further requires an intense faith in [human beings], faith in [their] power to make and remake, to create and re-create, faith in [their] vocation to be more fully human (... the birthright of all [people]). Faith in [people] is an a priori requirement for dialogue; the dialogical [person] believes in other [people] even before he [or she] meets them face to face. [This] faith, however, is not naive. The dialogical [person] is critical and knows that although it is within the power of [people] to create and transform in a concrete situation of alienation [people] may be impaired in the use of that power. Far from destroying [their] faith in [people], however, this possibility strikes [them] as a challenge to which [they] must respond. ... Without this faith in [human beings], dialogue is a farce which inevitably degenerates into paternalistic manipulation.

P. Freire (1972: 63-4)

References

Ekins, P. (1992). *A New World Order: Grassroots Movements for Social Change.* London: Routledge.

Freire, P. (1972). *Pedagogy of the Oppressed.* Harmondsworth: Penguin.

Freire, P. (1974). *Authority versus Authoritarianism,* an audio tape in the *Thinking with Paulo Freire* series. Sydney: Australian Council of Churches.

Fukuyama, F. (1992). *The End of History.* London: Hamish Hamilton.

Gramsci, A. (1971). *Selections from the Prison Notebooks.* London: Lawrence and Wishart.

Hall, S. (1982). Managing Conflict, Producing Consent. Unit 21 in Block 5: *Conformity, Consensus and Conflict of D102 Social Sciences: a Foundation Course.* Milton Keynes: Open University.

Hall, S. and Jacques, M. (eds.) (1989). *New Times: The Changing Face of Politics in the 1990s.* London: Lawrence and Wishart.

Harvey, D. (1989). *The Condition of Postmodernity.* London: Blackwell .

Held, D. (1987). *Models of Democracy.* Cambridge: Polity Press.

Hyland, T. (1994). *Competence, Education and NVQs: Dissenting Perspectives.* London: Cassell.

Jameson, F. (1991). *Postmodernism, or, The Cultural Logic of Late Capitalism.* London: Verso.

Johnson, R. (1979). Really useful knowledge, 1790-1850. In *Working Class Culture : Studies in History and Theory* (eds. J. Clarke, C. Critcher and R. Johnson). London: Hutchinson.

Milner, A. (1994). *Contemporary Cultural Theory.* London: UCL Press.

Mishler, W.T.E. and Rose R. (1993). *Reacting to Regime Change in Eastern Europe : Polarization or Leaders and Laggards.* Glasgow: University of Strathclyde.

Thomas, J.E. (1982). *Radical Adult Education : Theory and Practice.* University of Nottingham, Department of Adult Education.

Thomas, J.E. and Westwood, S. (eds.) (1991). *Radical Agendas? : The Politics of Adult Education.* Leicester: NIACE.

Thrift, N. (1986). The geography of international economic order. In *A World in Crisis* (eds. R.J. Johnson and P.J. Taylor). London: Blackwell.

Wiltshire, H. (1956). The great tradition in university adult education. *Adult Education,* XXIX, 2. Reprinted in *The Spirit and the Form* (ed. A. Rogers, 1976). Department of Adult Education, University of Nottingham.